The Law Says What?

Stuff You Didn't Know About the Law (but Really Should!)

Maclen Stanley

TCK PUBLISHING.COM

ISBN:
978-1-63161-180-3

Sign up for Maclen Stanley's newsletter at
www.maclenstanley.com/newsletter

Published by TCK Publishing
www.TCKpublishing.com

Get discounts and special deals on our best selling books at
www.TCKpublishing.com/bookdeals

Check out additional discounts for bulk orders at
www.TCKpublishing.com/bulk-book-orders

Table of Contents

Introduction

Back in the 1990s, PepsiCo ran a TV commercial advertising a point redemption program. Customers could collect "Pepsi Points" and redeem them for a variety of prizes. Most of the items were simple things like T-shirts (75 Pepsi Points) or sunglasses (175 Pepsi Points). But at the end of the commercial, an AV-8B Harrier II (a marvelous fighter jet capable of vertical takeoff and landing) suddenly landed in front of a school as a student emerged from the cockpit. Adorned in various Pepsi gear, he smirked at the camera as the text beneath him read: "Harrier Fighter Jet: 7,000,000 Pepsi Points."

You might have already guessed where this is going. Yes, someone actually tried to redeem their Pepsi Points for a fighter jet. Apparently, Kendall Jenner's ultra-cringy attempt to quell social unrest wasn't Pepsi's first advertising faux pas. When Pepsi refused to hand over a jet, the customer sued Pepsi for breach of contract and fraud. The United States District Court for the Southern District of New York, one of the most hallowed courts in the nation, ended up actually presiding over a case about a man with Pepsi Points who was upset over not receiving a fighter jet.

America!

Although the background might seem silly, the questions of law this case raised were actually quite interesting. The case examined the laws behind advertisements—more specifically, whether sellers are bound by the terms of their advertisements. Surprisingly, the answer was no. Although some exceptions exist, the law generally does not consider advertisements to be actual offers to sell advertised goods at the specified price or quantity, and a seller is under no contractual obligation to honor their advertisements. Instead, advertisements are thought of as merely "invitations to do business."

Most people probably assume that sellers must comply with their advertisements. Imagine a crotchety old man, flyer in hand, harassing the owner of an ice cream shop who won't sell him a scoop of rum raisin for the price advertised on the flyer. As it turns out, such a shop owner has no legal duty to make good on the advertised price of that disgusting ice cream.

After ruling that the Pepsi commercial did not amount to an actual offer, the court went on to explore the law even further. According to the court, even if advertisements were hypothetically considered actual offers, the particular offer for the fighter jet would still not be sufficient to form a binding contract. This is because offers must be "objectively reasonable" in order to be legally binding. Put simply, if it is clear that an offer is not actually serious, then no actual offer has been made. The court found that no reasonable person could have possibly believed that Pepsi's commercial *actually* offered customers a fighter jet. To thoroughly articulate the point that the offer was unreasonable, the court devoted five full paragraphs to explaining why the commercial was just a joke, offering in-depth analysis such as:

> "The callow youth featured in the commercial is a highly improbable pilot, one who could barely be trusted with the keys to his parents' car, much less the prize aircraft of the United States Marine Corps. Rather than checking the fuel gauges on his aircraft, the teenager spends his precious preflight minutes preening. The youth's concern for his coiffure appears to extend to his flying without a helmet. Finally, the teenager's comment that flying a Harrier Jet to school 'sure beats the bus' evinces an improbably insouciant attitude toward the relative difficulty and danger of piloting a fighter plane in a residential area, as opposed to taking public transportation."

A reminder: the court presiding over this case is widely recognized as the most prestigious and respected in the country, regularly handling high-profile matters that involve espionage, terrorism, and public corruption. And yet, here they were, trying their absolute damnedest to articulate why this Pepsi commercial about a fighter jet was a stupid joke not meant to be taken seriously.

I was introduced to this case in my class on contract law during my first semester at Harvard Law School. Having absolutely zero legal experience prior to attending law school, I was fairly taken aback by the case. I had always perceived the law as rigid and imposing—white men in black suits interpreting black-and-white rules and regulations, using words like "prima facie" and never allowing a single thought to float beyond the rigid confines of established legal parameters. This zany case not only upended that view, but also taught me some important, real-world lessons about the law. I quickly found myself thinking that other people, not just nerdy law students, would want to know about it too.

People should know that advertisements, in general, are not legally binding offers. Just because that Craigslist ad lists a First Edition Holographic Pikachu card for the shockingly low price of $19.99 doesn't mean that the seller has any legal obligation to actually give you the card for that price (or even sell it to you at all). And people should also know that offers made in jest likely won't hold up in court. We've all made a silly offer to a friend or family member, and whether it's telling your sister you'd give her one million dollars to fold your laundry or promising a friend you'd streak naked across the golf course if they sink that impossible putt, it's good to know that such offers aren't actually legally binding. This should make sense—no one should be legally obligated to own up to a sarcastic comment or playful joke.

As I continued to reflect on the many lessons in the fighter jet case, the beginnings of this book slowly sprouted to life.

The Purpose of This Book

The purpose of this book is twofold. The first goal is simple: to introduce you to the interesting, weird, and sometimes irritating things that you don't know about the law, but really should. The topics discussed in this book touch upon everyday life, whether because they involve laws that many people personally encounter, or because they are prevalent in national political discussions. The topics are organized into six global sections: (1) The Police, (2) Crime and Punishment, (3) Self-Defense, (4) Your Rights, (5) Employers and Landlords, and (6) The Court System.

Many of the laws discussed in this book will seem a bit weird. We've already examined a man's attempt to sue Pepsi for a fighter jet, but this was merely the tip of the iceberg. We will go on to discuss things like flipping the bird to police, setting booby traps in your home, and extraditing Dog the Bounty Hunter to Mexico. At one point, we'll even talk about ham sandwiches. This book will highlight just how quirky and bizarre the law can actually be.

Many of the laws in this book will also make you angry. In fact, the very first topic might infuriate you. Importantly, whenever we encounter a law that seems unjust or at odds with common sense, we will endeavor to understand the underlying rationales. Typically, there is a method to the legal madness—some kind of logic to support the law having ended up the way that it is. Seldom are judges, lawmakers, and lawyers seeking to make the world even more unfair. We will tackle these issues in several "But . . . Why?" sections throughout the book. Although you will be presented with detailed explanations of these rationales, it is ultimately up to you to decide whether they pass muster.

This brings us to the second goal of the book: to show you how to think like a lawyer. In law school, many students are surprised to find that they learn very little about the actual law (what lawyers refer to as the "black letter law"). It is only while studying for the bar exam—taken after law school to obtain their license to practice law—that students actually begin to memorize the various statutes and codes that govern society. This is because law school is designed to train students to think like lawyers, more so than to teach them the black letter law. Most often, courses will offer only the basic fundamentals of the law, or just enough for students to argue opposing views, question the law's theory, think about its history, and consider how it could be improved.

Keeping with this concept, this book will not bombard you with the innumerable minor details of our legal system. Trust me: there is absolutely no pleasure derived from reading page after page of nuanced judicial opinions, statutory text, and dense legalese (unless you are a certified weirdo). Rather, this book will paint you a broad picture of the most foundational tenets of the law. We will examine the Constitution and many of its Amendments, federalism, self-defense, the jury system, courtroom procedure, the differences between civil and criminal law, and much more. But even more importantly, we will continuously question and scrutinize the law, explore why it has evolved in these specific ways, discuss how it is actually applied, and question what form it might take in the future. In other words, we will think like lawyers do. Think of this book as bestowing you with a mini law degree. (Please don't actually flaunt this on your LinkedIn profile.)

It is my ultimate hope to fundamentally alter the way that you interact with the law. Armed with new knowledge, you'll enjoy a deeper understanding of the rationales that underpin the laws governing your life (however irritating or absurd), and better understand some of the "hot topics" you'll encounter on cable news or at the coffee shop.

Something interesting might also happen as you read this book. The Baader-Meinhof phenomenon, a recognized psychological illusion, occurs when you're confronted with a new topic, and suddenly that topic begins to surface everywhere in your life. This has likely happened to you before. Imagine that last week you were introduced to a new band by a friend. Now, you seem to notice that particular band *everywhere*: on the radio, on T-shirts, and on Spotify recommendations. Sound familiar? In reality, the band's presence isn't actually more widespread than it was before you learned about it; it's just that your selective attention now notices it among the myriad stimuli that inundate you at every moment of your life. The law is truly omnipresent, affecting every area of your life on a daily basis: from the health regulations ensuring that your morning bacon is free from foodborne pathogens, to the speed limit slowing your commute home, to the terms and conditions you signed before using your smartphone. After reading this book, I bet you'll begin to notice new legal insights and nuances in your own life where you may not have seen them before.

Finally, it is worth noting now, at the onset, that the law is inherently political—or, at least, *ideological*. It is no secret that one's opinion of any given law tends to align with one's political camp. For example, Democrats generally tend to favor gun regulations whereas Republicans tend to oppose them, and so on and so forth. But the law has even deeper roots. This is because the law sets the standards for those who *have* and those who *have not*. Land, money, access to goods and services, fundamental rights and privileges, and even basic freedoms— these are all shaped by the hands of the law. Throughout this book, I will aim to approach the law factually and in an unbiased manner, at least to the best of my imperfect human abilities.

The Comprehensive and Diligently Constructed Bibliography That No One Will Ever Read

Legal citations are pretty cumbersome. For example, the next case we're going to discuss is technically cited like this: Warren v. District of Columbia, 444 A.2d. 1 (D.C. 1981). Another case we'll discuss later on has the audacity to be cited like this: L.S. v. Peterson, No. 18-cv-61577, 2018 U.S. Dist. LEXIS 210273 (S.D. Fla. Dec. 12, 2018).

Doesn't look very pretty, does it? This book will only refer to cases by their title names (i.e., the cases above will simply read as <u>Warren v. District of Columbia</u> and <u>L.S. v. Peterson</u>). But do not fret: if you want to see the product of some very painstaking citation endeavors, they will all be listed in the bibliography at the end of this book. All cases, statutes, and relevant pieces of information referenced will be found there. This is likely of zero importance to anyone else, but I'm just trying to be professional here.

Quick and Dirty Definitions

In this book, you will learn about the law primarily through real-world cases and illustrative hypothetical examples. That said, there are a few foundational terms and concepts that are important to understand before we dive in:

Plaintiff: In civil lawsuits, the plaintiff is the one who commences a legal action. In other words, the plaintiff is the one doing the suing. By contrast, in criminal trials, it is the prosecutor, acting on behalf of the government, who brings a criminal charge. (Much more on civil versus criminal trials to come.)

Defendant: In both civil and criminal trials, the defendant is the one "defending" themselves, either against a lawsuit or a criminal charge.

Congress: Congress is the legislature of the federal government, meaning that its role is to make and pass laws. Congress is split into two distinct chambers: the House of Representatives and the Senate. In order for a law to pass, it must be approved by both the House and Senate through majority votes, and then signed by the President. Similar to the federal Congress, each state also has its own legislative body that makes and passes state laws. (We'll discuss federal versus state laws in depth later on.)

The Constitution: Drafted in 1787, you can think of the Constitution as the foundation of all American law. It even proclaims itself the "supreme Law of the Land," *because it is.* Although the Constitution is relatively short (at only 4,400 words), its breadth is immense: it organizes the structure of the federal government, defines and limits governing powers, outlines the relationship between the federal government and the states, and enumerates sacred liberties that are shielded from government intrusion. Over time, the Constitution has been amended. The first ten amendments cover some of the most important personal freedoms and are referred to collectively as the Bill of Rights. In total, the Constitution includes twenty-seven amendments (thus far!). In addition to the federal Constitution, each state also has its own constitution that outlines state-specific government policies and structures.

The Supreme Court: Regularly referred to as the "highest court in the land," the Supreme Court is the nation's ultimate tribunal. Its status as the *Grand Poobah* can be seen even in the way we reference it. According to legal writing guidelines, the "c" in "Court" should be capitalized only when referring to the Supreme Court. Furthermore, those who sit on the Court are referred to as "Justices," rather than mere judges. Currently, there are nine Justices on the Court, each appointed by the president and confirmed by the Senate. Interestingly, there is no actual rule requiring nine Justices, and there have been anywhere from five to ten throughout history.

The Supreme Court serves three main roles. First, the Court can review decisions from any other court in the nation that involve federal law or the Constitution. If the Supreme Court disagrees with that court's decision, it will be invalidated (i.e., overruled). Second, the Court can also review any action by the executive branch (i.e., the president) or legislative branch (i.e., Congress) to determine if it violates the law. If so, that action will be invalidated. Third, the Court has the final say in interpreting federal law, or any other law that implicates the Constitution.

You will see throughout this book the hugely important role of judicial interpretation. No written law can be completely comprehensive and cover every imaginable situation; indeed, the Founding Fathers explicitly worded the Constitution itself to be rather general, leaving it open to future interpretation as conditions changed. Most laws require someone to explain what they actually mean, particularly when applied to unusual situations. In our American legal system, this role is vested within the courts. All courts can interpret the law, but the Supreme Court gets the final say if any inconsistencies arise.

Finally, just as each state has its own constitution, every state also has its own supreme court, but all state courts must bow to decisions made by the federal Supreme Court. Again, we'll look at the supremacy of federal law compared to state law later in the book.

A Word of Caution

You know how you see all sorts of dumb warning labels on things? Like, McDonald's has a warning in big, bold letters on its coffee cups saying, "**CAUTION, handle with care, I'M HOT**." *No duh you're hot. You're supposed to be!* Well, this conspicuous warning exists because Stella Liebeck spilled a McDonald's coffee in her lap in 1992. She sued McDonald's and a jury awarded her more than five million dollars in today's dollars. Now, before anyone gets too envious of Liebeck's successful lawsuit, you should know that she actually suffered third-degree burns on 6 percent of her skin, including some *particularly sensitive* areas between her thighs. She spent eight days in the hospital undergoing treatment and multiple skin grafts. Liebeck's attorneys discovered that the coffee had resulted in such extreme burns because it was being served way too hot, at around 185-190 degrees Fahrenheit, which was much hotter than coffee from other restaurants.

This book needs a warning label too: **DO NOT TAKE ANYTHING YOU READ IN THIS BOOK AS ACTUAL LEGAL ADVICE.** State Bar codes and various attorney-client rules mandate that I make this point very clear. **THIS BOOK DOES NOT CONTAIN LEGAL ADVICE FOR YOU.** If you have a legal question or conundrum, stimulate the economy and contact a local attorney. This book seeks to provide a generalized overview of specific legal topics. There are fifty states in our country, each with their own unique book of laws. It would be a herculean (and boring) task to discuss every single law as it applies to each of the topics at hand. Things in the legal world can also change quickly and drastically. Depending on the year you're currently living in, it may have been a fair bit of time since this book's writing. So, when you learn later on how to legally shoot someone who's breaking into your house, for goodness' sake, please talk to a local attorney before you shoot anyone.

Phew. Now that we've gotten all of our ducks sufficiently in a row, let us get right into it.

SECTION 1: THE POLICE

The Police Have No Duty to Protect You
Special Relationships and the Duty to Protect

I live in Los Angeles, and at least once a day I happen across an LAPD patrol car. Emblazoned on each car is a familiar motto: "To Protect and to Serve." It's a comforting slogan, and one that I'm sure the vast majority of police officers dutifully abide by. But, to remain consistent with the actual law, the motto should really read: "To Protect and to Serve *If we feel like it.*"

Let's begin with a seminal case from the 1970s, Warren v. District of Columbia. Here are the facts:

In the early morning hours of March 16, 1975, Carolyn Warren and Joan Taliaferro were asleep in their third-floor apartment unit in Washington, D.C. Miriam Douglas was asleep on the second floor below. At around six in the morning, the entire building was awoken by the sound of the back door being broken down. Two men quickly forced their way into the second-floor apartment and began violently raping Douglas. Hearing the frenzied screams of their downstairs neighbor, Warren and Taliaferro immediately called the police. The emergency dispatcher assured them that help was on the way.

The call was dispatched to nearby officers as a "Code 2" response at 6:26 a.m. Although the jargon varies across different emergency departments, the Washington D.C. Metropolitan Police designate Code 2 responses as "pressing" but not time-critical responses, whereas Code 1 signifies time-critical situations and mandates the use of lights and sirens. Calls for a crime in progress are typically given a Code 1 response.

Frightened by the continued screams below them, Warren and Taliaferro had crawled outside a window and were huddled together on an adjoining roof as they waited for police to arrive. The two women watched a patrol car pull up their street and drive through the alley behind their house. Although the women never saw him, another officer later claimed that he had knocked on the front door of the apartment, but left after receiving no response. By 6:33 a.m., not more than just a few minutes after they had arrived, all police had left the scene.

But the attack on the second floor continued.

When Warren and Taliaferro made their way off the roof and back inside their apartment, they could still hear Douglas screaming. The women again called the police and requested that officers return to the scene. Once more, the dispatcher assured the women that help was on the way. But the second call was never actually dispatched to the officers.

Eventually, the screams stopped and several minutes of silence ensued. Now worried that their downstairs neighbor was dead, Warren and Taliaferro made what would turn out to be a grave mistake. The women called out to Douglas, thereby alerting the two men to their presence. The two men promptly forced their way into the upstairs apartment and ultimately held all three women captive for the next fourteen hours, during which they were robbed, beaten, raped, and forced to commit sexual acts upon each other.

Warren, Taliaferro, and Douglas (the "Plaintiffs") sued the District of Columbia and several members of the police department for negligently failing to provide adequate police services. Specifically, the Plaintiffs' claim of negligence included: the dispatcher's failure to forward the first call with the proper degree of urgency; the responding officers' failure to follow standard investigative procedures; and the dispatcher's failure to dispatch the second call entirely.

The court ultimately dismissed all of the Plaintiffs' claims, holding that the police officers and dispatcher had no legal duty to protect the Plaintiffs.

Infuriated yet? Let's unpack this a little bit.

I've seen many people cite this case as a way to imply that police *never* have *any* duty to protect *any* citizen at *any* time. However, the reality is more nuanced. What the court actually held in <u>Warren v. District of Columbia</u> was this: absent a "special relationship" between the police and an individual, no legal duty exists requiring the police to protect that individual. Here, the court found that no special relationship existed between the police and the Plaintiffs, and thus the police had no legal duty to protect them.

The duty to protect—or lack thereof—that the court applied to the police is actually the same standard that is applied to the average citizen. Generally, no one has a legal duty to assist, rescue, or otherwise protect someone else. In fact, this legally sanctioned apathy can stretch to pretty extreme lengths. In the famous case of <u>People v. Beardsley</u>, a married man was having an affair with a woman, whom he invited to his home while his wife was away. During her visit, the woman drank heavily and took several morphine tablets before eventually falling unconscious. Around the time that his wife was to return, the man asked an acquaintance to help move the lifeless woman into his basement in order to conceal her. The woman later died, and the man was charged with manslaughter for failing to render her aid . . . but he wasn't convicted. As explained by the court, while the man may have had a moral duty to protect the woman, the law imposed no such duty on him.

In other words, you can sit lazily along a riverbed, white wine spritzer in hand, and watch some guy (whom you don't know) get so distracted by his game of hacky sack that he unknowingly approaches a hungry alligator, gets dragged into the river, and is eaten by that alligator, all while you do absolutely nothing about it and face zero legal liabilities for your stone-cold heart.

However, the existence of a special relationship changes everything. Special relationships can legally obligate one party to protect another. As applied to the general population, special relationships typically exist when one individual is able to exert some level of control over another, such as a landlord has over a tenant or a parent has over a child.

In one interesting case from Tennessee, <u>Biscan v. Brown</u>, an intoxicated minor was severely injured in a car wreck after returning from a party at an adult's home. Because adults generally have some control over minors in their home (even if they're just guests), the court found that the adult had a special relationship with them. As a result of this special relationship, the adult had a duty to protect the minors, which included preventing them from driving while intoxicated. Thus, the adult was found partly responsible for the drunken wreck.

So, in reality, the result of <u>Warren v. District of Columbia</u> is not actually all that groundbreaking. All the court did was take the general duty to protect as it applies to the average citizen, and then extend it to the police (I'll explain why in more detail later).

The question still remains, though: What needs to happen to establish the kind of special relationship that will legally obligate the police to protect you? Unfortunately, the answer isn't very clear. As we have already seen, dialing 9-1-1 apparently will *not* create a special relationship. In fact, tons of cases, involving tons of upsetting details, have shown that courts can be quite reluctant to find a special relationship between citizens and the police.

For example, in <u>Hartzler v. City of San Jose</u>, Ruth Bunnell called the San Jose Police Department and reported that her estranged husband had just called her and told her he was coming to her house to kill her. She requested immediate police aid, but the department refused and told her she could call back once her husband had actually arrived. Approximately forty-five minutes later, the husband arrived at the residence and, true to his word, stabbed Ms. Bunnell to death. Ms. Bunnell had previously called the San Jose Police and reported her husband's violence more than twenty times prior to the night of her death. In at least one instance, the husband had been arrested for assaulting Ms. Bunnell. In a wrongful death lawsuit, Ms. Bunnell's family argued that, given the San Jose Police Department's familiarity with the situation, a special relationship existed between Ms. Bunnell and the police. However, the California court disagreed and held that no special relationship existed.

In the case of <u>Lozito v. City of New York</u>, Maksim Gelman went on a rampage through New York City, stabbing several people to death before arriving at a subway train. Gelman entered the train and homed in on his next victim, Joe Lozito. Gelman attacked Lozito, causing serious injuries, including deep stab wounds to Lozito's head and neck. Fortunately, because Lozito was highly trained in martial arts, he was eventually able to overcome and subdue Gelman after a violent struggle. Conveniently (perhaps *too* conveniently), NYPD officers arrived literally seconds later and took Gelman into custody. Lozito alleged that the NYPD officers had actually been in an adjoining subway car the entire time he was struggling with Gelman, watching as Gelman repeatedly stabbed him, but doing nothing until he had subdued Gelman himself. Lozito went on to sue the NYPD for failing to protect him. Although the judge expressed sympathy for Lozito, and found his version of events "highly credible," the New York court nevertheless dismissed the case, finding that no special relationship existed.

In <u>Davidson v. City of Westminster</u>, three women were stabbed in the same laundromat within one week's time by a man who appeared to be the same crazed assailant. The City of Westminster dispatched two police officers to conduct surveillance on the location. The officers saw Yolanda Davidson walk into the laundromat, followed soon after by a man matching the description of the assailant. The man entered and left the laundromat several times, arousing a great deal of suspicion, but the officers never warned Davidson. Minutes later, the man stabbed her. Only then did the police intervene. Davidson survived and went on to sue the police officers for failing to protect her. However, the California Supreme Court ruled that there was no special relationship between the officers and Davidson.

As we can see, establishing a special relationship between yourself and the police is not an easy endeavor. However, not all cases come out in the negative. Courts have certainly found such relationships to exist under some circumstances. Specifically, courts will find that a special relationship exists when the police have engaged in an affirmative act eliciting an individual's reliance. In simpler terms, a special relationship is created when the police have done something to cause an individual to rely on them.

For example, in Gardner v. Village of Chicago Ridge, James Gardner was a bouncer at a dance club. During an event at the club, he asked four rowdy individuals to leave. The four individuals apparently did not like this very much and proceeded to beat him up. Later that evening, police officers apprehended the four suspected attackers a few miles away. One officer returned to the club and requested that Gardner accompany him to where the suspects were being detained so they could be properly identified. At the scene, the police officers allowed the suspects to get too close to Gardner, and they ended up assaulting him once again. This time, Gardner suffered serious injuries before the police were able to restrain the attackers. An Illinois court held that the police had a special relationship with Gardner. Key here was the fact that the officer had requested that Gardner accompany him to where the suspects were located. In complying with the request, Gardner relied on the police to keep him safe from the dangerous suspects.

The Parkland Shooting

Before wrapping up this topic on special relationships, let us crystalize the issue by applying it to one final and tragic modern-day example. On Valentine's Day 2018, seventeen students from Stoneman

Douglas High School were mercilessly gunned down by Nikolas Cruz. As the full scope of the tragedy unfolded, the police response to the incident came under severe scrutiny. Allegations emerged that the deputies from the Broward County Sheriff's Office responded to the shooting in a slow, ineffective, and downright cowardly manner. Police did not enter the building until eleven minutes after the first shot was fired. Scot Peterson, the armed deputy specifically assigned to protect Stoneman Douglas that day, faced particular lambasting. After hearing shots ring out, Peterson never entered any buildings in an attempt to locate and neutralize Cruz. Rather, Peterson remained outside and appeared to hide for nearly fifty minutes after the shooting began. Video footage captured Peterson's inaction throughout the event.

Peterson (aka "The Coward of Broward," as locals have dubbed him) eventually resigned in disgrace. Peterson's inaction may have cost him his job and designated him a social pariah—but was his inaction also a basis for legal liability? Recently, a Florida lawyer representing students from Stoneman Douglas brought a lawsuit in federal court against Broward County, Broward County Sheriff Scott Israel, and several deputies, including Peterson. But the judge quickly dismissed the case, ruling that (you guessed it!) the police had no legal duty to protect the students of the high school.

But ... Why?

Okay, so ... why is it that the police don't have a duty to protect you?

The answer lies in pragmatics. In most of the cases discussed above, the victims got the short end of the stick. To think that a man can get stabbed nearly to death on a subway train while the police stand idly by just seems *wrong*. Still, there is an argument that offering these victims the justice they desired could have brought the entire government to a standstill. Indeed, when encountering a legal decision that seems totally at odds with common sense or morality, the underlying justification often involves, for better or worse, the pragmatics of things.

Many would argue that the creation of direct accountability between police officers and members of the community would catalyze an endless stream of lawsuits. Every victim of every crime would have a basis to bring a lawsuit against their local police officers for failing to protect them. Lawsuits and court proceedings are unimaginably slow and expensive, and even if the vast majority of these lawsuits were promptly dismissed, the amount of public time and money consumed in such court actions would be catastrophic to local governments. Many believe that this precious time and money is better spent developing resources and training police. Also problematic is the disincentive for qualified potential recruits. How many would still dream of becoming a police officer knowing that they could be dragged into court every time they failed to prevent a crime from taking place? Finding enough bodies to fill a diverse, well-adjusted, and competent police academy would be immeasurably more difficult than it already is.

By implementing the special relationship standard, courts have endeavored to strike a balance between *carte blanche* immunity for police inaction and the avalanche of lawsuits that would result from an express duty to protect. The law is often "grey" like this. Sometimes judges prefer to avoid the black-and-white or yes-or-no rules, and instead give themselves a bit of a grey area to tread upon when necessary. The problem with this, however, is that as the law becomes more grey, it also becomes more arbitrary, confusing, and susceptible to malfeasance. This is a theme you will continue to encounter throughout this book.

You Can Legally Flip the Bird to Police
First Amendment Protections

While we're on the topic of what the police don't have to do for you, let's take a quick look at something *you* can do to police! *All hail the First Amendment.*

Flipping the bird—or showing the middle finger—has a storied history. Those who study the gesture (apparently these people exist) trace its roots all the way back to ancient Greek texts. The Romans then adopted the gesture from the Greeks and carried it into their mainstream culture. In fact, Augustus Caesar once banished an actor from all of Italy for giving the finger to an audience member who hissed at him during a performance.

Today, flipping the bird is the most common of insulting gestures in the United States. Some people like to engage with the gesture more so than others. For example, a man named Robert Ekas from a small town in Oregon has a particular penchant for flipping the bird to every police officer he encounters. Although Robert claims he is merely making a "political statement," his gesturing often results in him being detained by the police and accumulating numerous citations for vague infractions like illegal lane changes and disorderly conduct. As it turns out, a recent federal case has made clear that retaliatory actions by the police in response to receiving the middle finger are illegal.

In 2017, in the town of Taylor, Michigan, police officer Matthew Minard pulled over Debra Cruise-Gulyas for speeding. But instead of writing Gulyas a "real" speeding ticket, Minard showed some leniency and wrote her a "non-moving violation" ticket. Most traffic tickets are "moving violations" because they happen when the car is, well . . . moving. By comparison, "non-moving violation" tickets also exist, which are typically related to parking violations or faulty equipment. Every so often, when police are feeling particularly generous, they will write non-moving violations for speeders because these tickets are much less expensive and usually don't add points to your license.

Apparently ungrateful for the reduction, Gulyas flipped the bird at Minard as she was pulling away from the traffic stop. Suddenly lacking in generosity, Minard pulled her over again, just one hundred yards away. He then amended the non-moving violation ticket into a real speeding ticket. Gulyas sued Minard, alleging that he violated her constitutional rights. Among other things, she claimed that he violated her First Amendment rights by retaliating against her in response to her protected free "speech."

Okay, it's time for a quick pit stop. In order to fully understand this case, we need to review the First Amendment. What better place for our first CRASH COURSE than the First Amendment?

CRASH COURSE

In these sections, which will appear frequently throughout the book, I will offer a brief rundown of the law in an entire area. The laws discussed in the CRASH COURSE will include some of the most important parts of our legal system, and they are just generally good for you to know about. I will always do my best to keep these sections lively and enjoyable because it's important that you read them.

The First Amendment

The First Amendment protects more than just verbal speech. As we are about to see, it also protects things like gestures and even some acts of symbolism, such as flag burning or wearing black arm bands to protest the Vietnam War. Beyond "speech," it also protects the freedom to practice the religion of your choice and prohibits the government from favoring or establishing a particular religion. Oh, and it also protects the freedom of the press and the right to peacefully protest. It's fair to say this single amendment packs quite a broad punch.

Critically, however, the First Amendment doesn't give you an unlimited right to say anything you want whenever you want to say it. This is a common misconception, as the freedom of speech is not absolute. Here are several categories of stuff you can't always say:

False Statements: Libel (written defamation) and slander (spoken defamation) are generally not protected by the First Amendment. In other words, you can't publish an article about your ex-boyfriend's non-existent case of antibiotic-resistant syphilis without facing some liability for it.

True Threats: True threats of physical violence are generally not protected, but it must be clear to a court that the threat is, in fact, true, and not just someone engaging in "trash talk" or hyperbole. There's one particularly notable example of the true threats exception: threats of violence directed at a former or current United States president can be a felony offense.

Fighting Words: Speech that is likely to make the person to whom it is addressed commit an act of immediate violence is not protected. The Supreme Court has defined "fighting words" as those that "by their very utterance inflict injury or tend to incite an immediate breach of the peace." For example, purposely antagonizing someone with racial slurs has been found to constitute fighting words. In contrast, flipping the bird and using colorful language such as "fuck you" generally has not been viewed as rising to the level of fighting words.

Incitement: Speech that incites lawlessness is also not protected. Importantly, the speech must be intended to provoke the imminent incitement of lawless action and be likely to actually provoke that action. The Supreme Court set this relatively strict standard in Brandenburg v. Ohio, which overturned the conviction of a Ku Klux

Klan leader who had been charged with incitement after he advocated for revenge against African Americans and Jews, and asked his supporters to march to Washington during one of his speeches. Since Brandenburg, speech falling under the umbrella of incitement is quite rare. Imagine someone has coordinated a protest on the steps of the Capitol Building because the price of Beanie Babies has gotten too damn high. The protest eventually turns unruly and pitchforks and torches are seen throughout the crowd. As the fervor builds, the leader of the protest suddenly announces: "It's time to burn the Capitol Building to the ground!" This would be prohibited incitement speech. By contrast, President Trump's comments during the rally that preceded the riots at the Capitol Building in early 2021 are more ambiguous in terms of incitement. The key questions here are whether Trump's remarks directed his supporters toward imminent unlawful action, and if his speech was likely to provoke such action.

Speech Owned by Another: The First Amendment won't protect you from stealing someone else's work (e.g., plagiarizing or infringing on copyrighted or trademarked work).

Lewd or Obscene Speech: Perhaps the least common exception, speech that is overly "lewd or obscene" is also not protected. Remember, "speech" can mean many different things under the First Amendment, including different forms of art, photography, and video. To be considered prohibitively lewd or obscene, the speech must have a "shameful or morbid interest in sex" and lack any "literary, artistic, political, or scientific value." Outside of clearly lewd and valueless things like child pornography, courts are extremely hesitant to restrain obscene speech.

Other Compelling Interests: As a final "catch-all" area, there will always be some competing government interests that must be balanced against free speech. Speech can be restricted if the government has a "compelling interest" in doing so. This is obviously a broad standard, so let's look at some examples. Compelling interests include things like prohibiting the dissemination of military secrets, imposing "gag" orders during trial, and preventing jurors from discussing cases outside of their deliberations. While some clear compelling interests exist, they are generally quite rare.

Finally, it is also critically important to understand that the First Amendment only prevents the government from restricting the speech of public citizens. Private individuals and private businesses can ban whatever type of speech they please. For example, during the COVID-19 pandemic, YouTube (a private company) removed from its platform several videos of scientists allegedly downplaying the severity of the virus and spreading misinformation. Although YouTube faced criticism for the censorship, its actions were perfectly legal. Unlike the government, private individuals and private businesses are fully entitled to retaliate against protected First Amendment speech. So, even if flipping the bird is considered free speech, you should think twice before doing it to your boss.

Returning to the case of <u>Cruise-Gulyas v. Minard</u>, the court ultimately ruled that Guylas' one-fingered salute was protected speech under the First Amendment. Thus, Minard violated Guylas' First Amendment rights when he (a government agent) retaliated against her for flipping him the bird. Because Minard had already issued the non-moving violation citation, it was clear retaliation for him to pull her over *again* and amend the citation to a real speeding ticket.

In 2020, the North Carolina Supreme Court in <u>State v. Ellis</u> also suggested that flipping the bird to the police was protected free speech. A police officer had stopped to help a stranded motorist out of gas during a snowstorm. Shawn Patrick Ellis was driving past the scene and, being the charming fellow that he is, decided to reach out his window and flip the officer the bird. In response, the police officer got into his vehicle and pursued Ellis for half a mile until he stopped. As justification for the traffic stop, the police officer claimed that Ellis was engaging in illegal disorderly conduct. However, the Supreme Court of North Carolina disagreed and ruled that the traffic stop was illegal.

Let's take a moment here and appreciate that we live in a country with some pretty great freedoms, like being able to flip off the police if and when we feel like it. In many other places in the world, this kind of stuff just wouldn't fly. For example, Russia recently passed a new law imposing steep fines just for verbally insulting the authorities. It's probably fair to assume that flipping off a Russian cop guarantees you a one-way trip to the Gulag.

Although many exceptions do exist, the law of the United States has generally championed the right to express opinions without government restraint. Many of our Founding Fathers actually believed that free speech was a prerequisite to a successful democracy. Democracies require an informed citizenry in order to cast votes truly in the best interest of the nation. In order to be appropriately informed, there must be no constraints on the free flow of information and ideas. A democracy cannot be true to its essential ideal if those in power are able to withhold information and retaliate against criticism.

No, the Police Don't Always Need a Warrant
Fourth Amendment Exceptions

Along with the First Amendment, the Fourth Amendment is among the most notable and influential laws of our nation. The Fourth Amendment protects the public from unreasonable searches and seizures by the government. Because citizens most often encounter searches and seizures through police action, we will focus our discussion primarily around law enforcement. However, it's important to understand that the Fourth Amendment applies to any agent of the government, not only the police. For example, a public school principal must abide by the Fourth Amendment when searching a student's locker, just as an OSHA (Occupational Safety and Health Administration) inspector must do the same while searching a business for workplace safety violations. Conversely, the Fourth Amendment is similar to the First Amendment in that its protections do not apply to actions by private individuals. A private employer can monitor emails sent on company servers or install security cameras in the office without worrying about the Fourth Amendment (although other relevant privacy laws might apply).

The unchecked governmental intrusion into the personal affairs of citizens was a problem the Founding Fathers took great lengths to try and preempt. In this spirit, the Fourth Amendment was written as follows:

"The right of the people to be secure in their persons, houses, papers, and effects, against unreasonable searches and seizures, shall not be violated, and no Warrants shall issue, but upon probable cause, supported by Oath or affirmation, and particularly describing the place to be searched, and the persons or things to be seized."

To protect against unreasonable government intrusion, the Fourth Amendment requires that warrants be issued prior to police conducting searches and seizures. We've all seen action shows on TV with police decked out in tactical gear, screaming "WE'VE GOT A WARRANT!" while pounding on the front door of some unsuspecting criminal. These are precisely the type of warrants required by the Fourth Amendment. Generally speaking, police receive warrants from a judge after providing satisfactory information showing that "probable cause" exists for the proposed search or seizure. We'll get to what "probable cause" means a bit later.

In addition to search warrants, warrants can also be required before making arrests (i.e., arrest warrants). As you might imagine, there are numerous exceptions to both warrant requirements. After all, police don't have to call a judge before making an arrest for DUI (driving under the influence), nor are they constrained from searching an individual's pockets when they see a baggie of marijuana sticking out.

Let's turn our focus now to discuss how these plentiful exceptions work in the real world, with particular attention paid to those among the most bizarre.

Arrest Warrants and Exceptions

"There's a warrant out for your arrest" is not a phrase that any member of the public wants to hear from a police officer. Imagine being pulled over for a simple speeding violation and, upon a search of your name in police records, you're informed by the officer that you have a warrant out for your arrest. *Uh oh.* You could have a warrant for a plethora of reasons, such as a missed court date, failure to pay child support, or even unpaid traffic tickets. With a warrant already issued, the police have the authority to immediately arrest you and take you into custody.

Successful criminal investigations typically end with a detective securing a warrant for the suspect's arrest. Often, law enforcement will investigate a case for several weeks or even months, documenting all evidence of criminal behavior before applying to a court for an arrest warrant. If a judge determines, based upon the evidence, that probable cause exists for the arrest, the warrant will be issued. With the warrant in hand, police can apprehend the suspect and take them into custody. Sometimes this is done with a large show of force, while other times the police peacefully take a suspect into custody without ever drawing their firearms.

A formal warrant is often the preferred method to initiate an arrest, but it is not the only option available. In fact, it is not even the most common. The vast majority of arrests are initiated out in the field, without any time to apply for a warrant or contact a judge. This is because police are able to skip the warrant process if they themselves have probable cause to make an arrest.

All right, it's time to discuss the actual meaning of probable cause! But don't get too excited—while probable cause is an extremely important legal term, it lacks a clear-cut definition. Generally, it means that an average police officer faced with a particular set of circumstances would reasonably believe that a crime has been—or is going to be—committed. Probable cause requires more than mere suspicion, but it also doesn't rise to the level of actual proof that a suspect is guilty. As with many things in the legal world, probable cause lands firmly in a grey zone, subject to extreme amounts of discretion.

Although warrantless arrests are valid based upon probable cause, there are still some special rules behind them. For example, even if the police have established probable cause that you have committed a crime, you generally cannot be arrested in your home without an arrest warrant. This is a lesser-known fact of criminal law, and it is based on the notion that the privacy of one's home is of ultimate sanctity. Still, don't think that simply hiding inside your house is a totally foolproof plan of escape. The law allows police to post officers outside a home to prevent a suspect from fleeing while a judge is contacted and an arrest warrant is issued. During work hours, it typically takes around three hours to procure an arrest warrant from a judge. But during weekends, late nights, or holidays, the process can take much longer, depending on the willingness and availability of the judge. Police can also enter into your home and arrest you without a warrant under any of these three important exceptions:

Hot Pursuit: If the police are in active pursuit of a suspect, they do not have to stop the pursuit just because the suspect ran into their home. For example, in <u>Gutierrez v. Cobos</u>, a police officer attempted to conduct a traffic stop on a vehicle driven by Anna Gutierrez. Gutierrez failed to stop, and the officer pursued her for several miles until she finally stopped at her apartment. Gutierrez fled from her vehicle and ran to the apartment door. A scuffle ensued as Gutierrez opened the door, and she was ultimately shot with a taser and arrested inside the apartment. Gutierrez sued the police officer, alleging that he unlawfully entered the apartment in violation of her Fourth Amendment rights. The federal court disagreed and ruled that the officer's entry into the apartment was justified under the hot pursuit exception. It is important to note that the pursuit must be actively occurring for this exception to apply. For example, the police cannot lose sight of a suspect in a chase and then turn up to their residence two hours later and attempt to enter without a warrant.

Danger to Others: If the police reasonably believe that someone inside a home is in imminent danger, they can enter and arrest a suspect. This exception is a logical one. Of course the police should not be restricted from entering a home where a potentially violent crime is actively being committed.

Consent: Although it's unlikely that a suspect will welcome the police into their home, if someone else consents to the police entry, the police can enter and make an arrest. However, not everyone has the legal ability to consent to a police entry. Generally, you can only consent to the police entering a residence if you have some authority over the premises. A suspect's roommate is an easy example of someone who is able to give consent. In contrast, the Supreme Court in <u>Chapman v. United States</u> ruled that a landlord cannot give consent for police to enter a tenant's apartment. Similarly, <u>Stoner v. California</u> held that hotel managers cannot give consent for police to enter into a guest's room.

Search Warrants and Exceptions

The government likes to suggest that it pays great respect to the Fourth Amendment. Over the years, the Supreme Court has continuously emphasized the grave dangers implicit in allowing government entities to conduct searches without warrants. In the famed Supreme Court case of <u>Katz v. United States</u>, the Court went so far as to proclaim that warrantless searches were illegal, "subject only to a few specifically established and well-delineated exceptions." Yet, the actual reality is very different. Numerous exceptions have come to undercut the search warrant requirement, with some of them being actually quite broad, ambiguous, and even a bit ridiculous. Below are some of the most common exceptions of today:

Consent: Just like the arrest warrant exception, police can conduct warrantless searches if someone with authority over the premises gives them consent to do so.

Hot Pursuit: As we already learned, if the police are in hot pursuit of a suspect, they can enter private property (i.e., anyone's home) without a warrant in order to pursue the suspect. If, while on the property, they notice evidence of a crime, the property can also be fully searched without a warrant. As an example, imagine that you and a friend live in a state where marijuana is illegal, but you decide to flout the law for the night and smoke a blunt in the comfort of your apartment. Everything's fine, life is easy, and your favorite musical tune is floating through the air like the wispy white clouds of a spring afternoon. But unbeknownst to you, down your apartment's corridor the police are chasing some kind of criminal. Suddenly, your door is kicked in and police flood your apartment, guns drawn. "He's not here!" one officer yells, as the blunt falls from your incredulous, open mouth. The police see the marijuana in your apartment, and you're charged with possession. As ridiculous as it might sound, a very similar situation occurred in <u>Kentucky v. King</u>, and the Supreme Court ruled that the search was valid.

Destruction of Evidence: Police are allowed to search a premise without a warrant if they reasonably believe that evidence is going to be destroyed. Here again, we find ourselves in a very grey area—what counts as a "reasonable belief?" Often, police are given pretty wide latitude. For example, in <u>United States v. Cephas</u>, a police officer received a tip that an individual named George Cephas was smoking marijuana in an apartment. The police officer knocked on Cephas' door and immediately smelled burning marijuana coming from inside. The officer asked Cephas for permission to come inside, and Cephas promptly responded by trying to slam the door in his face. The officer then pushed his way into the apartment and observed a marijuana "roach" in an ashtray. Cephas was ultimately arrested and later filed a lawsuit alleging that the officer had violated his Fourth Amendment rights by entering into his apartment without a search warrant. However, the court disagreed and found that the officer's actions were justified because he reasonably believed that the marijuana could be destroyed. The court rationalized their decision by explaining that marijuana is an easily destroyed drug, able to be ingested, burned, flushed, or washed down the sink.

Plain View: This exception is kind of redundant. A police officer can conduct a warrantless search of any item that is within his or her plain view (i.e., the officer can see the item). Literally speaking, if an item is actually in plain view, there isn't much of a search required. However, in real-world situations the plain view exception can get fairly complicated. For example, is an item still within an officer's plain view if they need binoculars or flashlights to see it? The case of United States v. Lee says yes. How about if the police can only see the item from the air via helicopter or airplane? In California v. Ciraolo, police rented a private airplane in order to fly over the home of an alleged marijuana grower. Officers flew over the house at an altitude of one thousand feet and quickly identified marijuana plants growing in the yard. The Supreme Court held that there was no violation of the Fourth Amendment because the search was part of the plain view exception.

As you can see, the plain view exception can be stretched to accommodate a wide breadth of searches. Still, there are limits. For example, in Kyllo v. United States, federal agents used a thermal-imaging device to scan the home of Danny Kyllo, a suspected marijuana grower. The agents believed that Kyllo was using high-intensity heat lamps to grow marijuana indoors. Indeed, the thermal imaging revealed areas of high heat throughout the home consistent with marijuana growing. The Supreme Court reviewed the use of the thermal-imaging device and found it to be an unconstitutional search in violation of the Fourth Amendment. Fundamental in the decision was the fact that thermal-imaging devices were not in common public use at the time this case was decided in 2001. Because thermal imaging was not commonplace, Kyllo had a valid expectation that his home would remain private from such devices. The Court's reasoning raises interesting questions regarding our rapidly developing technologies. Today, thermal-imaging cameras can be easily accessed on any smartphone by purchasing an inexpensive app. If the Supreme Court were faced with the same case today, would its decision in Kyllo be overruled now that thermal imaging is accessible to most everyone? That question has yet to be addressed.

Open Fields: The language of the Fourth Amendment makes clear that protections only apply to "persons, houses, papers, and effects." According to the Supreme Court in Hester v. United States, "open fields" do not fall under any of these categories. The precise definition of an open field isn't totally clear, but it generally means any open and undeveloped piece of land that is not actively used for living or business. Interestingly, a piece of privately-owned land can still be considered an open field even if fences and "No Trespassing" signs are clearly present. For example, in Oliver v. United States, Kentucky police received a tip that Ray Oliver was growing marijuana on his farm. (Are you sensing a theme here that police really don't like marijuana?) The farm was part of a very large field marked with "No Trespassing" signs. Without a warrant, police searched the field and found marijuana growing in it, about a mile away from Oliver's home. The Supreme Court ruled that the police were free to search what they described as an open field. Overall, it appears that only the land immediately surrounding one's home or business is protected by the Fourth Amendment.

Vehicle Searches: Police have much more flexibility in warrantless searches of vehicles compared to homes. Courts have relaxed the standards around vehicle searches for two primary reasons: (1) cars can be moved quickly, and thus, evidence can get destroyed while a warrant is obtained, and (2) people generally have a reduced expectation of privacy in a car compared to their homes. In order to search a vehicle without a warrant, the police only need probable cause that there is evidence of a crime inside the vehicle. This most commonly occurs with drug or firearm possession. For example, imagine a police officer pulls over a vehicle for speeding. As the driver rolls down her window, the officer smells a strong odor of marijuana. The officer now has probable cause to search the vehicle.

But there is another common avenue for police to conduct warrantless vehicle searches, and this one leads to a great deal of controversy. When police impound a vehicle, they are allowed to conduct "inventory searches." These inventory searches can be comprehensive and involve the examination of every compartment in a vehicle. Police don't need probable cause or even any suspicion that contraband is inside the car to conduct these types of searches. Courts have ruled that inventory searches are not protected by the Fourth Amendment because they are not actually undertaken for the purpose of gathering evidence. Rather, the purpose is to protect and catalog the owner's property, and to protect police from potential hidden dangers and claims for lost or stolen property. Paradoxically, however, evidence uncovered during these inventory searches can still be used against a defendant. This is particularly controversial because vehicles can be impounded by police for a variety of reasons, and during many arrests, including DUIs.

Drug-Sniffing Dogs: Over the decades, the Supreme Court has had the *ruff* task of analyzing the legality and predictive capabilities of a canine's snout. In Illinois v. Caballes, the Supreme Court ruled that the use of a drug-sniffing dog along the outside of a vehicle during a traffic stop is permissible without the need for any warrant or probable cause. Furthermore, an alert from a properly trained drug-sniffing dog can actually provide the probable cause needed for police to conduct a search inside the vehicle. You may have seen the police pull someone over and then call a canine to the scene when they suspect that the driver has drugs inside the car. The police officer will then run the dog around the exterior of the car. If the dog alerts to the presence of drugs, the officer then has sufficient probable cause to search the vehicle. Generally, this is a perfectly lawful practice. One important caveat, however, is that the police cannot unduly delay the traffic stop to wait for a drug-sniffing dog to arrive on scene. The dog must arrive within the reasonable timeframe of a normal traffic stop.

Police can actually use drug-sniffing dogs in more situations than just vehicle traffic stops. For example, they can generally be used in any public place, such as airports, parks, and parking lots. In Ohio v. Bryner, a police officer ran his drug-sniffing dog around an empty car sitting in a motel parking lot. After the dog alerted, the officer searched the vehicle and found illegal pills and other drug paraphernalia inside. The owner was then identified and arrested. By contrast, drug-sniffing dogs cannot be used to inspect the outside of someone's home without probable cause. Remember that the law often offers enhanced Fourth Amendment protections around one's home.

Border Searches: The areas around the borders of the United States, and also their functional equivalents such as international airports and ports, can be considered domains wherein Fourth Amendment protections fail to penetrate. Authorized by the very first Congress of the United States in 1789, customs searches in these areas require no warrant, no probable cause, and not even some degree of suspicion. Searches of persons, vehicles, and all items can be undertaken at will, for no particular reason at all. *Anything goes!* For example, in United States v. Flores-Montano, the Supreme Court ruled unanimously that CBP (Customs and Border Patrol) agents on the US-Mexico border could go so far as to remove and disassemble a vehicle's fuel tank to look for contraband, all without even needing any suspicion of wrongdoing. The rationale for this broad authority to conduct searches stems from the government's strong interest in protecting itself from foreign harms.

Things change—and also get more confusing—the further away from the border you travel. The Supreme Court in Almeida-Sanchez v. United States held that a warrantless search of an automobile by CBP agents twenty miles from the border without probable cause violated the Fourth Amendment. However, federal law states that CBP agents can, without a warrant, search vessels and vehicles for people without immigration documentation "within a reasonable distance from any external boundary of the United States." There are two important aspects here. First, the law only allows CBP agents to stop individuals and ask questions about their immigration status and documents; they cannot conduct an outright search of a person or vehicle without probable cause. Second—and criticized by many as problematic—a "reasonable distance" has been defined as one hundred miles from any United States border. This hundred-mile standard actually encompasses a massive majority of the population in the United States, due to the fact that most large metropolises are located on the nation's coastlines. In fact, two-thirds of the entire population resides within this zone. Some states, like Florida, actually lie entirely within the zone, and so their entire populations are impacted.

Stop-and-Frisk (aka "Terry Stop"): Stop-and-frisk policies reentered the public spotlight after former President Trump called for their strong revival in New York City. Since the 1968 Supreme Court case of Terry v. Ohio, police officers have been allowed to stop an individual on the street if they have a "reasonable suspicion" that the individual is involved in criminal conduct. If, during the stop, the police also reasonably suspect that the individual could be armed and dangerous, they may frisk the person—i.e., quickly pat down the outer clothing.

You might be asking: *What does reasonable suspicion mean? Is that the same as probable cause? What are all these ambiguous legal terms?!* The simplest answer is that reasonable suspicion is one step "below" probable cause, meaning that it is even more open to police interpretation and discretion. The Supreme Court has defined reasonable suspicion as requiring only something more than an "unarticulated hunch."

Let's look at the case of Terry v. Ohio to see why stop-and-frisk policies are so controversial. Here, a police detective observed several individuals acting suspiciously around a business (what the detective referred to as "casing" the building). Based on these observations, the detective had a reasonable suspicion of criminal activity and stopped the individuals. Believing that the individuals could be armed, he also frisked them. Two of the individuals were found to be illegally carrying concealed firearms and were eventually charged with felonies. Both were ultimately sentenced to more than one year in prison. This case demonstrates a situation in which the police did not have a search warrant, did not have probable cause that the suspects were armed, and did not have probable cause that anyone had even committed any crime, and yet police were still able to search the individuals, uncover firearms, and charge them with serious felonies.

Many believe that stop-and-frisk policies run afoul of the Fourth Amendment and afford police too much power to search citizens. Worse, many also believe that the easily satisfied requirement of reasonable suspicion and the large discretion granted to police creates the potential for racial discrimination. In 2013, New York City was sued for allegedly using stop-and-frisk policies as a discriminatory practice. The lawsuit pointed to data showing that over 80 percent of individuals stopped were African American or Hispanic. Since then, many cities have attempted to reform their stop-and-frisk policies in order to reduce the impact on minorities (although the practice itself still remains technically legal).

Despite the lawsuits and critiques, supporters of stop-and-frisk policies certainly exist, including many police chiefs, politicians, and Trump himself. Supporters often cite the correlation between the inception of stop-and-frisk policies and declining crime rates. However, the causal nature of this relationship has been disputed.

CRASH COURSE

Electronic Surveillance

As touched on in our discussion of thermal imaging searches, rapidly developing technologies have created interesting legal questions that the authors of the Fourth Amendment couldn't possibly have envisioned. Among those tactics defined as "electronic surveillance" are wiretapping, bugging, GPS tracking, data mining, social media mapping, and the monitoring of internet data.

Generally speaking, government electronical surveillance is considered a search under the Fourth Amendment and thus requires a warrant. For example, in the television show Breaking Bad, a DEA (Drug Enforcement Administration) agent, Hank, wishes to place a GPS tracking device on the vehicle of Gus, whom he suspects is a large-scale drug dealer. Hank knows he cannot legally place the GPS device on Gus's car without a warrant, so he asks Walt to do it instead. In the real world, simply asking Walt to place the GPS device on behalf of the DEA would not magically make it legal, but it at least shows that even television writers are aware of the restrictions the Fourth Amendment places on law enforcement.

These protections quickly dissipate, however, when foreign threats and national security interests are at play. An entire book could be written about the complex and ever-changing legal rules that govern the use of electronic surveillance as a tool for national security. The simple upshot is that intelligence agencies, namely the Federal Bureau of Investigation (FBI), National Security Agency (NSA), and Central Intelligence Agency (CIA), do not need a warrant to collect information on foreign adversaries and terrorists for communications that occur outside the United States. This should come as no surprise given that the Fourth Amendment, as part of the Constitution, offers no protection to non-citizens outside of the country. However, when electronic communications occur within the United States, or involve American citizens, intelligence agencies must use the FISA process, as described below.

It's important to quickly emphasize that Constitutional protections are still offered to non-citizens, so long as they are within the United States. In debates over immigration law, there is a pervasive misconception that the Constitution only protects U.S. citizens. In actuality, the Constitution specifies who its provisions apply to by referring to either "citizens" or "persons." While some provisions apply explicitly to citizens, such as the right to vote and run for political office, the vast majority of provisions apply to persons. Courts have interpreted the term "persons" to mean anyone within the United States, citizen or not.

A Unique and Highly Secretive Court System

In 1978, Congress passed the Foreign Intelligence Surveillance Act (FISA). FISA controls how the government can use electronic surveillance to collect intelligence from foreign agents suspected of espionage or terrorism. Foreign agents can include citizens of the United States, so long as there is evidence implicating them in international terrorism. FISA also created a special federal court system for the purpose of overseeing requests for foreign surveillance warrants—the Foreign Intelligence Surveillance Court (aka FISA Court).

The FISA Court has grown to be a source of near-legendary mystery. Under the guise of sensitive national security concerns, FISA Court proceedings are guarded with extreme secrecy. The confidential nature of the court, coupled with the fact that legislation passed after the September 11th attacks made FISA warrants much easier to secure, has led to great controversy. One of the few things we do know about the FISA Court is the number of warrant applications granted and denied. This data confirms what most have suspected: the court almost never denies a warrant request. Between 1979 and 2016, the court heard 39,654 applications for warrants and denied only 51.

At first glance, you might not find any inherent problems with the ease of securing FISA warrants. After all, these are potential foreign terrorists! While the theory behind the FISA Court might be to protect the United States from foreign adversaries, many argue that the real-world ramifications of these FISA warrants are not quite so hunky-dory. Consider the case of Carter Page, an American citizen and one of President Trump's former campaign advisers. The FBI obtained a warrant from the FISA Court to monitor the communications of Page (i.e., tap into his phone calls and emails) under the theory that he was acting as an agent of a foreign power: Russia. The problem here is that Page isn't talking exclusively to Russian contacts throughout his entire day. Presumably, Page is also talking to other American citizens, potentially those who have committed no wrongdoings, and in this case, potentially even the future president of the United States. In monitoring Page, the FBI likely picked up communications with numerous American citizens unrelated to any Russian affairs. This type of "incidental collection" is an inherent problem with FISA warrants.

Consider also the case of former National Security Advisor Michael Flynn. In 2016, FBI agents were secretly monitoring the communications of Russian Ambassador Sergey Kislyak. During their surveillance, a conversation with Flynn was incidentally recorded in which Flynn and Kislyak discuss sanctions that had just been levied against Russia for interfering in the 2016 presidential election. FBI agents later interviewed Flynn about the conversation, during which he lied about the fact that sanctions were discussed. Flynn ultimately pled guilty to felony charges for lying to the FBI. Trump pardoned Flynn before leaving office, but the case caused significant partisan controversy, particularly over the FBI's handling of the case and the incidental communications that were intercepted.

These two examples are far from isolated incidents. Many believe that such incidental communications happen with troubling frequency—and across all party lines. Technically, the government is supposed to undertake "minimization procedures" to protect American citizens from the incidental collection of data. For example, depending on the situation, the names of American citizens must be redacted, or the contents of communications destroyed. However, many exceptions apply, such as when the American person's name is necessary to fully understand the context of the foreign intelligence. Given the secrecy of the FISA Court and the ease of attaining FISA warrants, the public will likely never know just how much information is incidentally collected.

Let's Talk About Edward Snowden, Baby

No discussion of potential FISA abuses is complete without at least mentioning former-NSA contractor Edward Snowden. In June of 2013, Snowden leaked more than one million classified NSA documents to journalists after becoming disillusioned with the practices he observed while working with the NSA. Chief among the litany of information leaked was the revelation that the NSA was monitoring extraordinary amounts of phone records and nearly everything a user does on the internet. Snowden also showed that the NSA regularly spied on foreign leaders, such as German Chancellor Angela Merkel.

Although these NSA activities are condemned by most Americans, some of these actions might actually be compliant with the law. As we have already discussed, the NSA does not need a warrant to electronically surveil foreign actors on foreign soil. Thus, the NSA's monitoring of foreign leaders, while not exactly conducive to healthy foreign relations, does not violate United States law. Regarding the surveillance of American phone records, the Supreme Court has historically ruled that the Fourth Amendment does not prohibit the government from obtaining information that has been given to a third party. Here, third parties include telecommunication giants such as Verizon, Apple, AT&T, and the like. As the reasoning goes, when we use the phone, we know that we are conveying certain data to third parties and thus we "assume the risk" that this type of information might be divulged to the government. It's important to note that this so-called "third party doctrine" only applies to call logs (i.e., records of who called whom, when, and for how long). Listening to actual phone calls of American citizens is an entirely different matter that would (or should) generally require a warrant.

If the third-party doctrine strikes you as a bit ridiculous, you might be pleased to hear that it was recently found to be illegal. In September of 2020, a federal court in <u>United States v. Moalin</u> finally ruled that the NSA's massive collection of telephonic data violated the Fourth Amendment. While they acknowledged the third-party doctrine, the court found that the unprecedented scale and technological sophistication of the NSA's surveillance went beyond what the third-party doctrine had historically imagined. Snowden, who is still exiled in Russia, was actually credited by the court for exposing some of the NSA's improper activities. The NSA, for what it's worth, claims it no longer collects such data.

Exclusionary Rule

The exclusionary rule prevents the government from using evidence gathered in violation of the Fourth Amendment to prosecute a crime. Because of this, it is extremely important for police to follow each of the various rules that surround proper searches. One small mistake in search protocol can blow an entire criminal case, completely letting a criminal off the hook.

The exclusionary rule was formed in the seminal Supreme Court case, <u>Weeks v. United States</u>. Here, police entered the home of Fremont Weeks and found papers which were used to convict him of illegally transporting lottery tickets through the mail. However, during an appeal, it was revealed that the police had searched his home without a warrant. The Court went on to exclude the improperly collected evidence and dismiss the entire case.

The exclusionary rule actually reaches even one step further. An extension to this rule, termed the "fruit of the poisonous tree" doctrine, excludes from trial not only the initial evidence that was procured in violation of the Fourth Amendment, but also any other evidence that is derived from the illegal search. This has massive implications. Imagine that the police have wiretapped and recorded incriminating statements from suspected drug dealers without a warrant. One of the drug dealers says that he has hidden drugs and money in an abandoned warehouse across town. The police then visit the warehouse and recover these items. Not only will the illegally recorded statement (the poisonous tree) be excluded as evidence in a criminal case, so too will the drugs and money the officers found as a result (the fruit of that tree). As with everything in the law, there are some exceptions to these exclusionary rules, but for the most part, they provide a powerful deterrence to police misconduct.

Crossing County Lines Doesn't Mean the Police Will Stop Chasing You

Police Jurisdiction, The Hot Pursuit Doctrine, Citizen's Arrest

You're in rural Georgia and you're careening down a shoddy dirt road. Your knuckles on the steering wheel are whiter than a New England lacrosse team as you struggle to keep the car from rolling over. To your right, your cousin Bo is slapping his thighs as he cries, "Get to the county line!" Behind you, a curiously incompetent sheriff is licking his lips, yearning at the thought that—after all these tired years—he's finally going to catch you.

Up ahead, a wooden bridge emerges in the distance.

"That's it!" Bo roars. "That there bridge is the county line!"

"We're going to make it," you think to yourself as a wave of relief washes over you.

And then, suddenly, your eyes open. You awake to find yourself in your bedroom, curled up in your General Lee-themed racecar bed. That's right, you're thirty-seven years old and dreaming about *The Dukes of Hazzard* again. Maybe your dad was right about you. Worst of all, your dream was—legally speaking—totally inaccurate.

Hollywood writers seem to have some weird fascination with getting this particular aspect of the law wrong. *The Dukes of Hazzard* is far from the only offender. Countless shows and movies suggest that if you cross a city, county, or state line, the police pursuing you will be repelled by some kind of magical forcefield. This simply isn't correct. So, to the up-and-coming screenwriter reading this book, please don't indulge the same illegitimate trope for the one thousandth time.

CRASH COURSE

Let's first begin by talking about the different kinds of police and the various jurisdictions that they cover. There are generally four "levels" of law enforcement agencies: the city, the county, the state, and "the feds."

City Police: The city police are who you think of when you imagine a regular cop. These are the everyday police that patrol your city and respond to 9-1-1 calls. Some cities have behemoth-sized police forces. For example, the NYPD employs nearly forty thousand officers. This is due primarily to the city's enormous population, but also its potential as a target for terrorist attacks. On the other hand, some cities, such as Ellendale, Delaware, have historically employed only a single police officer.

For you college students, you may have noticed that your campus has its own police force. While many students might look at campus police as being "lesser" than your regular city cop, this is an inaccurate assumption. Campus police are sworn officers just like all other members of the police. They usually go through the same training, attend the same academies, and pass the same tests. As such, they can carry weapons, make arrests, and enforce the law just the same as city police officers—sometimes they actually operate as a wing of the local city department. Now, if you happen to attend a smaller school, your campus may only have private security guards. As much as they might like to be, these security guards are *not* the same as local police. In addition to campus police, there are numerous other sworn officers with full police authority who have jurisdiction over particular areas, such as airport police and transit police.

County Police: The county police are most commonly referred to as "Sheriff's deputies." This is because most state constitutions require that counties elect a local sheriff whose job is to keep the peace and enforce law and order. The elected sheriff then employs deputies to work under his or her authority. Some people find it odd that the head of county law enforcement attains their job via an election process. While this can seem a little strange, you might rest easier knowing that most counties at least require candidates for sheriff to have law enforcement experience and meet minimum educational qualifications before mounting their election campaigns.

The sheriff typically has jurisdiction throughout the entire county, including all cities, villages, and townships. In many rural areas, there are no city police, only the sheriff and the state-level police (discussed next, hold on!). Many sheriffs focus their efforts primarily on areas that are not adequately policed by local city authorities. Sheriffs are also typically responsible for managing county jails and security at county buildings, such as courthouses.

State Police: Every state has some kind of state-level police force. These state police forces focus on either statewide traffic enforcement, general law enforcement and investigation, or both. Different states will divvy up these responsibilities differently, sometimes across multiple agencies. For example, Georgia has the Georgia State Patrol, whose focus is largely on enforcing traffic laws on the state's highways. However, Georgia also has the Georgia Bureau of Investigation ("GBI"), whose purpose is to investigate crimes. Similarly, the Texas Rangers, adorned in their famous cowboy hats, ties, and western boots, investigate crimes from cattle theft to major homicides, while the Texas Highway Patrol focuses on the enforcement of state traffic laws. Massachusetts, on the other hand, has the Massachusetts State Police, whose duties serve both functions: they patrol major roadways throughout the state and perform criminal investigations.

"The Feds": The federal government also has numerous law enforcement agencies. You've probably already heard of the more notable agencies, such as the FBI (Federal Bureau of Investigation), ICE (Immigration and Customs Enforcement), DEA (Drug Enforcement Administration), and Secret Service. These agencies have jurisdiction throughout the entire country, so long as violations of federal law are involved.

Most people are unaware that nearly every federal agency includes some type of law enforcement division. For example, the United States Postal Service has a law enforcement wing—the Postal Inspection Service. Postal Inspection agents enforce over two hundred federal laws related to crimes involving the postal system, its employees, and its customers. Each year, these agents make over five thousand arrests, primarily for crimes such as mail theft, mail fraud, and illegally mailing drugs and weapons. Interestingly, these agents have a reputation of being some of the most dedicated and intelligent in all of federal law enforcement. Even the IRS (Internal Revenue Service) and EPA (Environmental Protection Agency) have law enforcement divisions with gun-carrying federal agents capable of making arrests for violations of federal tax and environmental law.

Bigger Doesn't Always Mean Better

It goes without saying that the federal government is bigger than a state, a state is bigger than a county, and a county is bigger than a city. But the police agency with the larger jurisdiction doesn't necessarily wield more authority. This is another popular trope that doesn't correspond to legal realities—the FBI doesn't just waltz into a crime scene and push the local police aside like some kind of law enforcement royalty. In fact, the FBI doesn't even have any jurisdiction if the crime involves state laws, which comprise the vast majority of criminal offenses (the difference between state and federal criminal law will be discussed more thoroughly in the next section of this book). More often, different police agencies strive to work together. Indeed, joint task forces, in which police from multiple types of agencies work together, have only become more common. Federal agencies are particularly fond of forming task forces with local police, and even go so far as to temporarily deputize the local police as federal agents while working on the task force. Many believe that combining federal agents (with their more expansive resources) and local police (with their intimate knowledge of local affairs) makes for a particularly effective crime-fighting team.

It's easy to see why most people think police don't have authority outside of their designated city, county, or state. After all, it's literally in the name. Does the San Francisco Police Department really have power outside of San Francisco? In some states, such as California, the answer is actually always yes. All California police officers, no matter their city or county, have authority throughout the entire state. Specifically, a sworn police officer who is in uniform and driving a vehicle equipped with an emergency light and siren can effect a traffic stop or make an arrest anywhere in the state. In one reported instance, two San Bernardino police officers were being trained to ride motorcycles at the California Highway Patrol Academy in Sacramento, four hundred miles from their hometown. While in uniform during one of their training rides, they spotted a purse snatcher in the act. They chased the suspect down and arrested him. When the suspect eventually noticed the officers' San Bernardino uniforms, he curiously asked, "Hey, what are you guys doing in Sacramento?"

Although a California police officer can technically enforce the law anywhere in the state, they usually don't want to. Arresting an offender outside the officer's typical zone of work means that the officer has to correctly identify the court for that area, cite the offender to that court, and likely return to that court in order to eventually testify during the prosecution. It's much more common for police in these situations to simply contact the local department in order to effectuate a traffic stop or arrest.

California is one of the few exceptions in terms of affording police statewide authority. In most states, it's true that police only have authority in their designated city, county, or state. However, even in these states, there is a special legal doctrine that allows police to cross into other jurisdictions so long as they are actively pursuing a suspect. Yes, the hot pursuit exception returns!

The Hot Pursuit Exception

You may remember from our previous discussions that the hot pursuit exception allows police to sidestep some Fourth Amendment protections when they are in active pursuit of a suspect. As it turns out, it also allows police to enter into jurisdictions other than their own. In nearly every part of the country, a police officer can follow a suspect outside of their designated jurisdiction if they are in hot pursuit. At the city and county level, most jurisdictions have agreements in place allowing officers from neighboring cities and counties to cross into their jurisdiction when chasing a suspect. At the state level, many states have passed hot pursuit laws explicitly allowing out-of-state officers to enter their state in order to make arrests. For example, Maryland's hot pursuit law reads:

> "A member of a state, county, or municipal law enforcement unit of another state who enters this State in [hot] pursuit and continues within this State in [hot] pursuit of a person to arrest the person on the ground that the person is believed to have committed a felony in the other state has the same authority to arrest and hold the person in custody as has a member of a duly organized State, county, or municipal corporation law enforcement unit of this State . . ."

These hot pursuit laws and agreements are numerous and often differ in language and scope. Nevertheless, the ultimate result of these laws is the same: police can cross jurisdiction lines when chasing a suspect. In other words, *The Dukes of Hazzard* lied to you.

The hot pursuit exception should make intuitive sense. After all, criminals should not be afforded such easy avenues of escape by simply crossing a line on a map. If this were the case, imagine the risks for any shopkeeper, homeowner, or business that happened to be located near a jurisdictional boundary. Miscreants would flock to these areas to commit their crimes and make a quick getaway.

While the hot pursuit exception might apply to the majority of the country, it's important to note that it will not extend outside of it. Hollywood portrayals of criminals fleeing national boundaries are actually fairly accurate. As you learned during your second-grade geography class, the United States only borders two different countries.

In Canada, American police have no authority to enter the country, even while in pursuit of a suspect. In 2010, a Maine State Trooper who was unfamiliar with the border area accidentally pursued a suspect into Canada's New Brunswick province during a high-speed chase. After a few miles, the trooper realized that she was in Canada and quickly stopped the pursuit and returned to the United States. The trooper was disciplined and suspended for two days without pay.

Likewise, American police have no authority to enter into Mexico. That said, the reality for suspects attempting to flee into either Mexico or Canada is that the lack of American police authority is usually of little consequence. American police agencies adjacent to national borders are trained for the potential that suspects will attempt to flee into the neighboring country, and they are very familiar with the protocols for contacting the neighboring country's border patrol officers. These foreign border agents will set up roadblocks and get ready to apprehend the suspect once they arrive at the border. As the old adage goes: no matter how fast you drive, you cannot outrun a radio.

Furthermore, the United States has extradition agreements with both Canada and Mexico. This means that most suspects apprehended by these foreign governments will simply be returned (or "extradited") to the United States for prosecution. As we have discussed, Edward Snowden still remains safely in Russia because Russia and the United States do not have an extradition agreement. Quite a few countries don't have extradition agreements with the United States, such as Cambodia, China, Ethiopia, Indonesia, Iran, Libya, Morocco, Rwanda, Senegal, Somalia, Sudan, Syria, Uganda, Ukraine, Vietnam, Yemen, and more. As you might have noticed, these countries are among those with which the United States has not fostered great relationships.

The extradition agreements between the United States and Canada and Mexico are bilateral, meaning that the United States must also comply with requests from Canada and Mexico to extradite individuals (yes, even American citizens) back to these countries if they have committed serious crimes within their borders. Back in 2003, the television star Dog the Bounty Hunter was famously arrested by U.S. Marshals at the request of the Mexican government. Earlier in the year, Duane "Dog" Chapman had traveled to Puerto Vallarta, Mexico and captured Andrew Luster, a U.S. citizen and serial rapist who had fled the country after posting a $1,000,000 bail in California. Due to Dog's actions, Luster was ultimately turned over to Mexican authorities and extradited back to the United States to face a 125-year prison sentence. However, Dog had a problem: bounty hunting was illegal in Mexico and criminal charges were filed against him. Dog quickly returned to the United States, but Mexican officials requested that he be extradited to Mexico to face trial. After his arrest by the Marshals, Dog was allowed to remain in the United States while diplomatic negotiations took place between the two countries. Eventually, four years later in 2007, Mexican officials finally agreed to drop the charges and the saga concluded.

CRASH COURSE

Let's begin this CRASH COURSE with a law school-style exam question.

Fact Pattern: Suppose a city police officer works in a state that does not afford him statewide authority. Today, he's due to testify at the county court. In order to get to the courthouse, the officer must travel through a neighboring city. While driving in the neighboring city, he happens upon an armed robbery in progress. A man in a hooded sweater is pointing a gun at a frantic grandma and demanding her gold necklace. Immediately, the officer jumps from his car, does a barrel roll, tackles the suspect, and places him under arrest.

Question: Given that the officer was *not* in hot pursuit, and that he was outside of his jurisdiction during the arrest, was the arrest lawful?

Answer: Yes! Even without any official police authority, the officer can still make an arrest. Do you feel bamboozled? You should! As surprising as it sounds, all citizens—not just the police—can make arrests, under the right circumstances.

Citizen's Arrest

A citizen's arrest is an arrest made by a private citizen, i.e., any person who is not acting in the capacity of a sworn law enforcement officer. This practice dates back to medieval England, during which authorities encouraged ordinary citizens to help apprehend criminals. Thus, even when the police find themselves out of their jurisdiction and without any authority, they can still effect an arrest in their capacity as a private citizen. Here, an "arrest" really just means to physically detain an individual until a police officer with proper authority arrives, and then the power of the arrest transfers to the officer.

Today, all states have laws authorizing private citizens to make arrests. The scope and breadth of these laws differ by state, but most allow for a citizen's arrest under one of two scenarios: (1) the arresting citizen didn't see the crime occur but has a reasonable belief that a felony was committed, and the felony *actually was committed*; or (2) a suspect is actively committing any crime (felony or misdemeanor) *in the presence* of the arresting citizen.

Okay, that was a lot of words, but it's really important that you paid attention to them, particularly the italicized bits. There are some very important things to discuss here regarding the high risks involved in making a citizen's arrest. But, before jumping into that, we need to make certain we understand the difference between a felony and misdemeanor. Misdemeanor crimes are "lesser" crimes compared to felonies. Examples of misdemeanor crimes include things like public intoxication, petty theft, some forms of drug possession, and trespassing. Felony crimes generally encompass more serious crimes and carry higher penalties. A good (but not universal!) rule of thumb is that crimes carrying penalties in excess of one year in prison are felonies.

Now, back to citizen's arrests. Imagine you own a store, and upon a visit to your building, you see that one of the storefront's windows has been broken. In an alley around the corner of the store, you notice a group of incriminating-looking youths with bricks in their hands. Naturally, you assume they have broken your window, and so you chase them down, catch one of the suspected perpetrators, and physically detain him (i.e., effect a citizen's arrest) while calling for police.

Was this a lawful citizen's arrest? Well, it depends. The crime was not committed in your presence, so a lawful citizen's arrest will require that you had a reasonable belief that a felony was committed, and that a felony was actually committed. Given the proximity of the suspected perpetrator to the broken window and the compelling evidence of a brick in his hand, you had a reasonable belief that a crime was committed—but was it a felony? In most states, certain monetary thresholds must be reached before vandalism switches from a misdemeanor to a felony. In California, vandalism must cause damage in excess of $400 to be considered a felony; anything less is a misdemeanor. Suppose the broken window only amounts to $395 in damage, meaning that the perpetrator you arrested only committed a misdemeanor. *Uh oh.* In this case, you have falsely imprisoned this person and can now be subject to your own criminal charges or a civil lawsuit (we'll talk more about the differences between criminal and civil actions in the next section).

Finally, it's worth noting that shopkeepers have their own special right to temporarily detain customers whom they reasonably believe have stolen from their store. This "shopkeeper's privilege" even allows shopkeepers to use reasonable force, if needed, to detain a suspected shoplifter. A few important rules do apply, such as: the detention must occur on or very near to the premises of the store; the amount of force used to effectuate the detention must be reasonable; the detention can only last for a reasonable amount of time; and the purpose of the detention must be solely to discover if the suspect has actually stolen from the store (as soon as that question is answered, the detention must stop). The shopkeeper's privilege can also transfer to employees of the store, such as security guards. However, many corporate policies forbid employees and security guards from ever using force in order to detain a suspected shoplifter, even when it may be legal to do so. The potential for injuries and the huge liability risks involved in using physical force simply outweigh the cost of stolen goods.

SECTION 2: CRIME AND PUNISH-MENT

It Doesn't Matter if You Thought She Was 18
Statutory Rape, Strict Liability Offenses

Thus far, we have examined some very grey areas of the law. For example, due to the "special relationship" standard, the law offers a large amount of discretion and subjectivity when analyzing whether the police have a duty to protect. The concepts of probable cause and reasonableness are also greyer than George Clooney's marvelous hair. Now, to contrast these areas of significant ambiguity, let's talk about a type of legal liability that is completely black and white. The question of guilt depends on one thing and one thing only: *did you do it?* If yes, you're guilty—no ifs, ands, or buts.

This type of liability is referred to as "strict liability" because, well . . . it's strict. Like your parents. *Your curfew is at midnight! I don't care if your car breaks down, you spontaneously combust, or you are abducted by aliens—you will be home by midnight or you're GROUNDED!*

Most crimes are not strict liability offenses. Indeed, most crimes require a specific mental state along with the actual physical criminal act. That might sound confusing, so let's break this down with a CRASH COURSE.

CRASH COURSE

Mens Rea

Mens rea (Latin for "guilty mind") refers to the state of mind required to convict a particular defendant of a particular crime. Even if the defendant actually committed the act, they cannot be convicted of a crime unless they committed the illegal act with the required state of mind. The *mens rea* requirement is premised upon the idea that one must possess a guilty state of mind to be convicted of a crime. Put very simply, your brain has to be just as culpable as your body. Famed Supreme Court justice Oliver Holmes illustrated this concept way back in 1909 when he stated, "even a dog knows the difference between being stumbled over and being kicked."

Generally, the *mens rea* for crimes are organized hierarchically, into the following four levels:

(1) Acting purposely: having the express intent to commit the act. Example: An offender sets an explosive package right outside the front door of the White House with the express intent of killing the president. As the president steps outside, the offender detonates the package and the president is killed.

(2) Acting knowingly: knowing that your conduct would cause a particular result. Example: An offender places the same explosive package outside the front door of the White House. He detonates the explosive and the president is killed, but so too are several of the Secret Service agents standing near to him. The offender did not have the express intent to kill the Secret Service agents, but he knew that the explosion would kill them too.

(3) Acting recklessly: completely disregarding a substantial and unjustified risk. Example: An offender places the same explosive package outside the front door of the White House. This time, he does not wish to actually kill anyone, but wants to detonate the package as a point of protest. He explodes the package when no one appears to be nearby, but ends up killing several people standing just behind the front door.

(4) Acting negligently: you don't know of the risk, but you should have been aware of it. Example: A person is visiting the White House on a tour when a shady looking man in a black trench coat and mask hands the visitor a package. "Place this outside the front door of the White House," the man instructs in a thick Russian accent before running away. Finding the man odd, but not actually concerned, the visitor does as he is told and places the package outside the front door. The package is later detonated and the president is killed. The visitor was not actually aware of the risk that the package was a bomb, but probably should have been.

Let's look at how *mens rea* works in the crime of murder. Murder is often defined by statute as taking a human life purposefully or knowingly. Imagine it's a rainy day. You and countless others are walking down a sidewalk beside a busy main road on your way to work.

Suddenly, you slip on the wet sidewalk. As you fall, you slam into the person walking beside you and knock them into oncoming traffic. The person is hit by a bus and instantly killed. Well, that totally sucks, but you aren't going to be convicted of murder (and neither is the bus driver, for that matter). You did not purposely or knowingly kill that person. Because this was just an honest accident, you did not possess the required "guilty state of mind," or *mens rea*, to be convicted of murder.

Now, imagine the same scenario, but this time your very dumb friends have challenged you to wheelie blindfolded on your bicycle down the entire length of the same sidewalk. About halfway across, you lose your balance, fall down, and knock the same person into the path of the Death Bus. What happens now? You still didn't purposefully or knowingly kill this person, so murder charges likely won't stick. However, the prosecutor might charge you with a "lesser" crime, such as involuntary manslaughter, which usually requires a *mens rea* of negligence. It would be up to the prosecutor to prove to the jury that you should have known that your blindfolded wheelie risked killing someone on that busy sidewalk (i.e., you were negligent).

The *mens rea* forms an exceedingly important area of the law. When individuals envision a criminal trial, they likely imagine a prosecutor trying to persuade a jury that a defendant has committed a particular act. While this can be true, a significant portion of the trial is also usually devoted exclusively to examining the defendant's mental state at the time of the act.

As another example, the crimes of possessing or distributing narcotics typically require some kind of knowledge on the part of the offender. As an example, the federal Controlled Substances Act makes it an offense to knowingly possess a controlled substance. If charged with such a violation, crying to the judge that you thought the marijuana was just oregano for your pizza might actually be a valid defense, though a jury would need to believe your story.

Overall, the vast majority of crimes in our penal codes require that some kind of mental state be included with the act. Crimes that involve strict liability, such as statutory rape, are rare exceptions.

———————————————•◆•———————————————

Statutory rape is generally defined as sexual intercourse with a person who is not of the legal age to consent. And under many states' legal codes, it is a strict liability offense. It does not matter if you had no intention of having sex with an underaged person, if you had no knowledge of their actual age, or if you wholeheartedly and reasonably believed that your sexual partner was actually of legal age. If they were underage and you had sexual contact with them, you're guilty. Full stop. No exceptions.

Let's examine a real-world example:

In 2015, Zach Anderson, a nineteen-year-old from Indiana, met a girl from Michigan on the app "Hot or Not." The two struck up a virtual relationship and, eventually, Anderson drove all the way to Michigan to meet the girl. During their in-person *rendezvous*, the two had sex. This whole time, the girl had been telling Anderson that she was seventeen, and Anderson had no reason not to believe her. The girl was physically developed and was said to have the maturity of someone easily that age. She had even registered in the "adults" section of the app where they first met. As it turns out, however, she was only fourteen years old. The age of consent in Michigan is sixteen years old. *Yikes.* Because the sexual act took place in Michigan, Anderson was subject to Michigan law. The girl eventually confessed to her parents that she'd had sex with Anderson. Her parents promptly notified the police, who coordinated an effort to arrest Anderson across the state border in Indiana.

Anderson was arrested and pled guilty to Michigan's statutory rape law. He spent seventy-five days in jail. He was also sentenced to five years of probation, during which he was forbidden from using the internet, owning a smartphone, or having any contact with anyone under the age of seventeen (save for immediate family). Perhaps worst of all, he was placed on the sex offender registry until 2040. For several reasons, the case garnered a great deal of national attention. First, the girl had explicitly misled Anderson about her age. Second, the girl was physically developed, which gave Anderson the reasonable belief that she was seventeen years old, as she claimed. And third, the girl's parents actually had a change of heart and came to defend Anderson, asking the judge for leniency during his sentencing. Importantly, although it is often the parents who first alert police that a statutory rape has occurred, neither the parents (nor the victim) have the power to later stop criminal charges once they have been filed by the prosecutor. If the government gets involved in a crime, they run the show. The parents went so far as to start a Change.org petition seeking to have Anderson's charges dropped, which received almost two hundred thousand signatures nationwide.

But all of this was to no avail. Michigan followed a strict liability approach to statutory rape. Because Anderson was nineteen and the girl only fourteen, he was guilty. Full stop. No exceptions.

But ... Why?

What makes statutory rape different? Why is it a strict liability offense? Here, the general aim of courts and lawmakers, whether right or wrong, has been to protect children and adolescents. When the safety and well-being of young people is at issue, more draconian rules of law tend to apply.

In enforcing strict liability for statutory rape, numerous judges and lawmakers throughout the decades have articulated what they believe to be significant potential harms caused by sexual activity involving children and adolescents. Among these are physical harms (risk of venereal diseases, especially HIV), social harms (such as pregnancies, which result in economic consequences), and emotional harms (psychological distress). For some, the potential harm to young people involved in sexual activity outweighs the harm done to those who have strict liability imposed on them.

But perhaps the biggest factor supporting strict liability is its massive deterrent effect. In the world of criminal law, there are generally four philosophical rationales for punishment: retribution, rehabilitation, incapacitation, and deterrence. The theory of retribution aims to offer a sense of satisfaction and contentment with the law to victims and society by giving a wrongdoer "what they deserve" (i.e., their "just deserts"). This may prevent future crime between the victim and perpetrator by appeasing the desire for personal avengement. The rehabilitation approach tries to prevent future crimes by altering a criminal's behavior in a positive way. Incapacitation aims to prevent future crimes by simply removing criminals from society. Finally, the theory of deterrence posits that future crimes can be prevented by frightening would-be criminals with risks of harsh consequences.

With regard to statutory rape, deterrence is accomplished by placing the risk of an error in judgment (regarding a sexual partner's age) with the offender. If statutory rape laws were not strict liability offenses, but instead required a *mens rea* of purpose, knowledge, recklessness, or negligence on the part of the offender, many would argue that children would not be as protected from sexual predators. Such predators could legally maneuver their way out of criminal charges more easily.

Finally, a few courts have also justified strict liability by focusing on the emotional effect that a trial for statutory rape might have on the victim. If statutory rape offenders were allowed to introduce evidence of the victim's older appearance and maturity level, trials would likely transform into drawn-out presentations focusing on every aspect of a victim's looks, dress, attitude, intelligence, and all those personal things that a victim of a sexual crime certainly does not want put under a microscope.

The Defense of Mistake

While many of the statutory rape laws in this country are strict liability offenses, it's important to mention that several states have begun altering the status quo and now allow a defendant to avoid criminal liability if they made a reasonable mistake about the victim's age. It was California who first catalyzed this trend in 1964 in People v. Hernandez. Here, the defendant had engaged in sex with a girl who was seventeen years and nine months of age, but the age of consent in California was—and still is—eighteen years. Operating under the paradigm of strict liability, the defendant was initially denied the opportunity to present evidence showing that he reasonably believed the girl was actually eighteen (i.e., that he had made a reasonable mistake). However, the court quickly reversed course and ruled that the defendant should be allowed to present such exculpatory evidence. Importantly, the court stressed that the mistake must be reasonable—i.e., "in good faith." The defense of mistake cannot apply if an offender engages in sexual intercourse with a victim who is clearly underage. Today, about twenty states allow the defense of mistake. Other states have also adopted what are colloquially referred to as "Romeo and Juliet Laws." These laws prevent serious criminal charges against young people who engage in consensual sex with others close to their own age, typically for differences less than three years. (To be clear, "consensual sex" is a redundant phrase. All sex is consensual; if not, it is rape. I use the term here only for clarity.)

Statutory rape laws provide a perfect example of just how much the law can vary state by state. Not only does the age of consent range between sixteen and eighteen across the country, but a reasonable mistake as to a sexual partner's age can also be either a total defense to criminal liability or utterly inconsequential, all depending on what border you happen to be within. Returning to the case of Zach Anderson, recall that he lived in Indiana and drove to Michigan to meet the girl, thus subjecting himself to Michigan law. Had the girl instead met Anderson in his home state of Indiana, he would have likely avoided all legal consequences. Indiana allows for the defense of mistake, whereas Michigan does not. Indeed, the simple act of crossing a line on a map can truly mean the difference between freedom and a life-altering criminal sentence.

CRASH COURSE

How can different states be so... *different?*

You may have heard before that the United States isn't actually a true democracy, but rather a federal republic. A lot of this boils down to semantics, but generally a democracy can be defined as a government in which laws are made by the majority of voting citizens. In a republic, laws are made by representatives chosen by the people, with the law-making power of these representatives held in check by some kind of official charter (e.g., the Constitution). Many would argue that the United States is much more akin to a republic. In fact, the word "democracy" never actually appears in the Declaration of Independence, the Constitution, or any of the main founding documents of our country.

As goes the Pledge of Allegiance: "I pledge allegiance to the Flag ... and to the **Republic** for which it stands ..."

But the United States also practices something called federalism. Federalism is a system of government in which the same territory is controlled by two levels of government. It is one of the most important aspects of our entire country's rule of law. In the United States, the federal government provides one level of power, generally responsible for broad governance of large nationwide issues. The independent state governments provide the second level of power, and generally govern issues of more local concern. Thus, citizens of the United States are always subject to two different autonomous governing bodies, each with their own powers to make laws. This is in contrast to a central or unitary government, in which one central power governs the entire country. About half of all countries around the world practice some kind of federalism.

While the Supremacy Clause of the Constitution mandates that federal law is superior to state law—meaning that any federal law will invalidate a conflicting state law—the Constitution also makes clear that federal law only applies to a limited number of areas. As such, the power of the federal government is both limited and supreme: limited to those powers granted to it by the Constitution, but supreme within that sphere.

Because federal law is limited to only certain areas, state governments end up wielding significant power. The Tenth Amendment provides that all powers not delegated to the federal government under the Constitution are reserved for the state governments. In simpler terms, if the Constitution does not explicitly articulate that the federal government has power over something, it means the state governments do. The Constitution generally leaves open to the states the power to regulate the health, safety, and general welfare of their inhabitants. This means that most criminal laws (such as statutory rape) are left entirely to the states to enact and enforce.

Because states have the power to enact their own laws, different states with different political compositions and demographics of citizens (and therefore, different political compositions and demographics of representatives who pass laws) will naturally have very different laws. Gun laws provide a good example of such state-to-state variance. In order to purchase a handgun in California, you must pass a safety test, obtain a permit, register the firearm with appropriate documentation, limit the gun's magazine size to ten rounds of ammunition, and wait ten days after the purchase to actually receive the gun (this is referred to as the "cooling off period," and its purpose is to prevent those in hotheaded arguments from immediately being able to access a firearm). In Kansas, literally none of those things are required; you can purchase a handgun without a test, permit, registration, or waiting period. Magazine size is also unlimited, and citizens are even allowed to carry their handgun in public (both open carry and concealed carry are allowed).

Overall, the concept of federalism was at the heart of our country's inception. Many of our Founding Fathers believed that the surest way to maintain individual liberty was to instill safeguards against centralized power. Giving states their own power to govern offers citizens the opportunity to move to different areas with laws that embody their personal views. Citizens also have more input (and proximity) with the representatives making decisions on their behalf. At the same time, a centralized federal government is necessary for things such as ensuring national security, engaging in foreign affairs, and regulating an economy. Federalism strikes an important balance between individual liberty and a strong government.

You Can Be Tried for the Same Crime Twice
Double Jeopardy, The Dual Sovereign Doctrine

Now that we understand the fundamentals of federalism, it's time that we examine some very important differences between federal crimes and state crimes. Every state has its own set of criminal laws, and so too does the federal government, which technically covers the entirety of the United States. Violations of state criminal laws are generally prosecuted in state courts, whereas violations of federal criminal laws are prosecuted in federal courts. Sounds simple enough, right? The vast majority of criminal prosecutions in the country are violations of state law and take place in state courts. For context, about thirty million criminal cases are tried in state courts each year, while only around one million take place in federal courts. State legislatures have the power to criminalize just about any action within their state (referred to as "police powers"), so long as the law does not violate the rights granted in the United States Constitution or in their own state constitution.

Federal criminal laws are made by Congress and, in theory, the Constitution requires that these laws relate to some federal or national nexus (more on this later). This nexus can take many forms. For example, criminal actions that cross state lines are considered federal issues. Thus, mail fraud is typically a federal crime, as is a kidnapping that involves transporting the victim from one state to another, and crimes that occur on commercial airliners. Other crimes are federal because they take place on federal land, involve federal property, or affect individuals within the federal government (for example, a rape in a national forest or an assault against a U.S. Senator). Finally, some crimes are inherently federal in nature because they involve the United States as a whole, such as counterfeiting money, immigration fraud, or espionage.

Federal criminal prosecutions are typically more involved than state criminal cases. Ever heard the expression, "Don't make a federal case out of it"? The point here is that the federal government usually doesn't prosecute someone unless they are prepared to throw the full weight of the United States (and its vast resources) behind the case. Federal criminal cases are investigated by some of the most renowned law enforcement agencies in the world (such as the FBI) and prosecuted by some of the country's most accomplished attorneys (who come from the ninety-three United States Attorney's Offices throughout the U.S. and its territories). For many lawyers, becoming a federal prosecutor is considered the pinnacle of their career.

In state courts, state prosecutors are often overworked and underpaid. In stark contrast, federal prosecutors typically have a much lower caseload, and they can actually work alongside federal law enforcement agents as the case develops. By the time an individual has been charged with a federal crime, the federal prosecutor has likely been investigating them for months and already secured warrants from a federal judge for things like wiretaps, GPS monitoring, phone records, and credit card statements. According to data from the Administrative Office of the U.S. Courts, less than one percent of individuals charged with a federal crime go to trial and win their case.

Double Jeopardy

Although federal and state laws are distinct, it is often the case that both sets of laws cover the same action. For example, there is a murder law under the federal criminal code and a murder law under every state's criminal code. In many instances, the actual language in the statutes is identical. This is where things can start to get confusing.

Imagine your "average" murder in the state of Nebraska. Let's say an abusive husband one day returns home from work and finds his wife having an affair with the neighbor. In a fit of rage, the husband ends up killing his neighbor with the shotgun in his closet. No federal issues are implicated here, so the state murder law is the only appropriate avenue through which to bring a prosecution.

Now, in contrast, imagine someone murders a mail carrier in the state of Nebraska. Because the mail carrier is a federal employee, a federal nexus now exists, making federal murder charges appropriate. However, state murder charges would also still apply because the mail carrier was murdered within Nebraska. Although it rarely happens, there is technically no rule forbidding the prosecution of an offender in both state and federal court for the same criminal act, assuming it violates both state and federal law.

"But what about double jeopardy?!" You are no doubt screaming, fists raised in the air.

Indeed, the Fifth Amendment of the Constitution prohibits the prosecution of the same crime twice. Specifically, it states: ". . .[N]or shall any person be subject for the same [offense] to be twice put in jeopardy of life or limb . . ." This "double jeopardy clause," as it has been dubbed, has historically served two purposes. First, it ensures the significance and validity of an acquittal at trial (i.e., being found not guilty). The clause prevents the government from essentially being able to "try again" if they lose a case. Additionally, it protects citizens from the financial and psychological trauma that would accompany multiple trials for the same offense. The prohibition against double jeopardy is actually one of the oldest legal tenets in Western society, dating back to 355 BC, when Athenian politician Demosthenes declared: "The law forbids the same man to be tried twice on the same issue."

Yet, despite the clear language of the Fifth Amendment, the Supreme Court has created a special "dual sovereign doctrine" that allows federal and state governments to both pursue charges for the same crime, even if this means that a defendant would effectively be prosecuted twice. Interestingly, the doctrine also allows for multiple states to prosecute a defendant for the same crime. For example, in <u>Heath v. Alabama</u>, Larry Heath traveled from his home state of Alabama to Georgia, where he hired two men to kill his wife for two thousand dollars. Heath then returned home with the men, who killed his wife as instructed. Georgia authorities charged Heath with murder and he received a sentence of life imprisonment after pleading guilty. However, shortly thereafter, authorities from Alabama also charged Heath with murder and sought the death penalty. Because the murder was solicited in Georgia, but completed in Alabama, both states possessed valid jurisdiction to prosecute the murder under their own laws. Heath attempted to argue that the double jeopardy clause prohibited him from being convicted in Alabama since he had already been tried in Georgia for the same crime. Relying on the dual sovereign doctrine, the Supreme Court disagreed, and Heath was ultimately tried, convicted, and executed in Alabama.

The only caveat with the dual sovereign doctrine is implicit in the name—the criminal charges must be brought by different governments (or "sovereigns"). The federal government cannot prosecute an individual for the same crime twice, nor can any single state do so.

Fortunately for would-be offenders, the dual sovereign doctrine is rarely invoked. The general consensus among prosecutors is that the governing body responsible for bringing charges, whether state or federal, is competent to ensure adequate justice. In fact, the United States Justice Department has a written policy discouraging federal prosecutors from bringing charges if a state government has already done so. Put simply, prosecutors don't like to step on each other's toes.

However, this is not to say that the dual sovereign doctrine never comes into play. It sure does—but most often only when certain social elements are at play. Let's look at another example:

In 2010, Roberto Miramontes Roman allegedly shot and killed Deputy Sherriff Josie Greathouse Fox in Utah. Deputy Fox had stopped Roman on a rural road in Millard County for suspicion of drug trafficking. In his attempts to evade arrest, Roman allegedly shot Deputy Fox two times with an AK-47 and left her to die in the middle of the road. Roman was an undocumented immigrant with a lengthy and violent criminal record, and had previously been deported several times. Deputy Fox was the first female law enforcement officer in Utah to be killed in the line of duty. Suffice it to say, political tensions in this case were sky-high.

State authorities in Utah brought charges against Roman. He initially confessed to the murder of Deputy Fox but later recanted his story during his trial in state court. In what came as a huge shock to local law enforcement and the surrounding community, the jury ended up finding Roman not guilty of Deputy Fox's murder.

But Roman's legal journey did not end there—less than twenty-four hours after Roman's acquittal, the Millard County Sheriff's Office contacted federal prosecutors and asked for their help. The U.S. Attorney's Office in Salt Lake City and the Federal Bureau of Alcohol,

Tobacco, Firearms and Explosives (ATF) quickly began their own investigation. Federal prosecutors eventually brought eleven charges (including murder) against Roman. Prosecutors were able to establish a federal nexus to the murder charge because Roman allegedly murdered Deputy Fox in an attempt avoid arrest for interstate drug trafficking. This brought his actions under the umbrella of federal jurisdiction (remember, a crime that takes place between states is a federal offense). As you might have already imagined, federal prosecutors are keen to make creative arguments implicating federal jurisdiction where you might not think it overtly exists.

During Roman's trial in federal court, ATF firearms experts used ballistic evidence to reconstruct the shooting scene and demonstrate to jurors that Roman had been the shooter. This was new evidence that the state prosecution was apparently unable to deliver. On this go-around, the jury unanimously found Roman guilty of Deputy Fox's murder. And in 2017, nearly five years after his acquittal in state court, a federal judge sentenced Roman to life in prison.

Throughout the trial, Roman's lawyer vigorously argued to the court that his second prosecution on federal charges amounted to inequitable double jeopardy. According to Roman's lawyer, prosecutors were given an unfair "test run" in state court and were able to learn from the defenses he offered there. Nevertheless, the law was clear, and the federal judge allowed the trial to continue without much hesitation.

When prosecutors from a different sovereign elect to undertake a second prosecution, it is typically in order to quell social outrage, right a perceived wrong, or secure political points. The murder of Deputy Fox is emblematic of the precise scenario in which the federal government would elect to intervene: a female law enforcement officer is murdered by an undocumented immigrant, the local community is in an uproar, and the state prosecutors ostensibly gaffed and failed to secure a conviction for a defendant who had previously confessed to the murder.

Consider another example—perhaps the most famous—in which the dual sovereign doctrine was applied. In 1992, the LAPD officers who were filmed violently beating Rodney King were acquitted in a state court outside of Los Angeles (in the historically conservative and majority-white suburb of Simi Valley). The acquittals sparked the infamous LA Riots, which lasted six days and resulted in the deaths of sixty-three people. Not long thereafter, federal prosecutors brought charges for civil rights violations against the same officers in federal court. Two of the officers were found guilty and sentenced to more than two years in prison.

Dylan Roof, the white supremacist and mass murderer who killed nine people attending a church in South Carolina, was the first person to ever face the death penalty at both the state and federal levels. The State of South Carolina charged Roof with nine counts of murder, for which he faced the death penalty as a possible sentence. The federal government also charged Roof with thirty-three different crimes, eighteen of which carried the death penalty as a possible punishment. (Federal charges were appropriate because Roof had committed hate crimes, and all crimes committed because of a victim's race, gender, religion, or national origin are subject to federal enforcement under the Hate Crimes Prevention Act.) Roof ultimately made a deal with South Carolina and pled guilty to the state charges in order to avoid being sentenced to death. However, he was still sentenced to death by lethal injection at his federal trial. He currently sits on death row at the United States Penitentiary in Terre Haute, Indiana.

But . . . Why?

Many are left to wonder why the Supreme Court has even allowed the dual sovereign doctrine to exist, given its questionable encroachment into Constitutional protections. The rationale of the dual sovereign doctrine is actually quite simple and hinges upon the definition of "offense." As mentioned, the text of the Fifth Amendment's double jeopardy clause prohibits a defendant from being "twice put in jeopardy of life and limb" for "the same offense." For decades, the Supreme Court has believed that an "offense" is defined as a wrongful act under the laws of a particular sovereign. If there are two sovereigns (i.e., a state and the federal government), and the same act implicates the laws of each, then there are two separate offenses, which makes any double jeopardy protections inapplicable. As interpreted by the Supreme Court, the text of the double jeopardy clause implies that a defendant is only protected from being tried twice for the same crime by the same sovereign.

While the Supreme Court's semantic argument might not seem very convincing to some, it's important to reflect on the real-world application of the dual sovereign doctrine. Removing any political or emotional bias from the cases we've discussed, the question remains: should a defendant really be subjected to a second prosecution simply because the crimes they have allegedly committed are politically charged, newsworthy, or because prosecutors in their first trial made some kind of mistake? Does this align with your version of justice?

Think critically about the dual sovereign doctrine. If you were a prosecutor, would you utilize it? While opinions regarding thorny issues in the law tend to follow political leanings, this isn't one of those situations. Conservative thinkers might have approved of the doctrine in the case of Deputy Fox's murder, while more liberal minded individuals might have advocated for it during the prosecution of the police officers in the Rodney King trial. Indeed, in the 2019 Supreme Court case Gamble v. United States, in which the Supreme Court once again upheld the dual sovereign doctrine, the two dissenting justices (i.e., the justices arguing for the doctrine to be overruled) were Ruth Bader Ginsburg (a notoriously liberal democrat) and Neil Gorsuch (a republican conservative). It has become an unfortunate rarity for Supreme Court Justices on opposite sides of the political aisle to vote in the same manner.

You Can Be Found Guilty of Murder without Ever Killing Anyone
The Felony Murder Doctrine

I still vividly remember sitting in my criminal law class and first being introduced to the concept of felony murder.

"You can be found guilty of murder without actually killing anyone," my professor began her discussion.

Felony murder applies when someone commits a certain kind of felony (typically those categorized as "inherently dangerous") and someone else dies in the course of that felony. If that happens, any offender involved in the felony can face murder charges. It generally does not matter if the death was accidental or if the offender did not actually do the killing.

In order to understand how extreme this law really is, it's helpful to conceptualize it with an example. Here's the exact hypothetical that was first presented to me in law school:

Imagine two people, Amy and Bob, have agreed to rob a liquor store. Amy is the getaway driver and parks outside the store while Bob goes inside to demand money. Bob is using a BB gun instead of a real firearm, and promises Amy that he has no intention of harming anyone inside. During the commission of the robbery, the elderly store owner is so frightened by Bob that he suffers a heart attack and dies. Because robbery is a felony, both Amy and Bob can face felony murder charges.

As extreme as this hypothetical example may seem, real-world defendants have been charged with murder under very similar circumstances. In <u>People v. Ingram</u>, a man was convicted of murder after the owner of the home he was burglarizing died of a heart attack. In <u>State v. Rodriguez</u>, a getaway driver was convicted of murder after her three accomplices to a home burglary were shot and killed by the homeowner, who was armed with an AR-15 rifle. Perhaps it is worth emphasizing again: her accomplices were shot by the homeowner, but she still got convicted of their murders. To implicate felony murder, the requisite death need not be of a victim of the crime; any death can suffice. As one last example, in <u>People v. Hernandez</u>, the defendant attempted to rob an undercover police officer during a drug sting operation. A violent struggle ensued as several other officers arrived on the scene. The defendant allegedly pointed a gun at one of the officers, prompting that officer to shoot at him; but in the hysteria, the officer missed the defendant and struck another officer in the head, killing him. The defendant was convicted of the police officer's murder.

Felony murder departs significantly from the conventional scope of murder. You'll remember from our previous discussions that a mental component (or *mens rea*) is required of most crimes. Murder typically requires that the defendant either purposefully or knowingly killed the victim. But with felony murder, the offender's mental state regarding the killing is completely ignored; all that matters is that a death occurred during the commission of a felony.

Like statutory rape, you may be thinking that felony murder is another strict liability offense. While this might be a keen observation, it's not totally correct. Historically, felony murder has not been considered a strict liability offense. This is because a mental component is still required during the commission of the underlying felony. According to many legal scholars, when a defendant commits a felony that is inherently dangerous, he or she does so knowing that some innocent victim may die. This mental state is imputed to the subsequent murder. Under this reasoning, it becomes very difficult to justify a conviction for felony murder when the underlying felony is not inherently dangerous. As such, the vast majority of jurisdictions limit the felony murder doctrine to dangerous felonies that create a foreseeable risk of violence or death (e.g., rape, robbery, arson, burglary, etc.).

Many of you are undoubtedly thinking that felony murder is quite draconian and unfair. If so, take solace in knowing that you aren't alone—felony murder is one of the most widely criticized features of American criminal law. For decades, significant activism has targeted the repeal of felony murder laws. In particular, a great deal of criticism has focused on the disproportionate impact these laws have on young minority populations. Indeed, some studies have shown that African American and Hispanic first-time offenders form the majority of those affected by felony murder laws. Because neuroscience has shown us that the brains of adolescents and young adults are not yet able to fully appreciate the future consequences of risk-taking, many have argued (albeit unsuccessfully) that the felony murder doctrine violates the Eighth Amendment's prohibition on cruel and unusual punishment when applied to young offenders. Perhaps most striking, the Supreme Court, in Tison v. Arizona, actually upheld the use of the death penalty in felony murder cases. The only caveats are that the defendant must have been a significant participant in the underlying felony, and the underlying felony must have been inherently dangerous to human life. Thus, an individual can actually be sentenced to death without ever killing anyone!

Today, the United States remains the only developed country in the world to still follow the felony murder doctrine. Even the United Kingdom (where the doctrine was created) abolished it in 1957. In total, forty-four states and the federal government include some form of the felony murder doctrine in their legal codes.

But . . . Why?

Given the extremely controversial nature of felony murder, let's take a moment to see if we can make sense of the reasoning behind it.

One of the most common justifications for the felony murder doctrine is that it deters dangerous felonies from occurring. This logic is simple: when potential murder charges are involved in the commission of a felony, offenders might think twice before committing the criminal act at all. While many regular citizens might not know about felony murder laws, career criminals are often well aware that they exist. The doctrine has also been rationalized as affirming the unique sanctity of human life. By definition, a felony that results in a human death is more serious than one that does not. Accordingly, an act that results in a death should be punished more severely, regardless of the intent to actually kill.

For many of you, the above justifications might not be up to snuff. But perhaps pause for a moment and imagine that someone you love is the victim of a felony murder. Return to the hypothetical of Bob and Amy robbing the liquor store. Imagine your father is the store owner who suffers a deadly heart attack during the robbery. Would your perception of these laws change? After all, if not for Bob and Amy's felonious attempt to rob your father, he would still be alive.

Now, let's push your viewpoints even a bit further. In the summer of 2020, our nation clamored in uproar in response to a video depicting the shooting and killing of Ahmaud Arbery in Satilla Shores, Georgia. Arbery, a twenty-five-year-old Black male, was reportedly jogging in his community when he was followed by two white men, Gregory and Travis McMichael. The McMichaels contend that Arbery had just committed a burglary in the neighborhood, and that they were following him in order to effectuate a citizen's arrest. The McMichaels, armed with shotguns, pursued Arbery in their truck until a scuffle ensued and Travis McMichael shot Arbery dead. The McMichaels were eventually charged with murder—but not "regular" murder. No, it was felony murder. Let's look at why.

Like many murder statutes, Georgia's murder law requires that the offender intentionally causes the death of another. Although virtually everyone found the circumstances surrounding Arbery's death abhorrent, the reality is that it would be extremely difficult for the prosecution to prove that the McMichaels intended to kill Arbery, particularly to a rural, largely white, and largely conservative Georgia jury. Right or wrong, the defense attorney at trial would vigorously argue that the actual intention of the McMichaels was to stop Arbery and effect a citizen's arrest while waiting for police to arrive—not to kill him. The prosecution knew this, and thus opted instead to charge the McMichaels under Georgia's more expansive felony murder law. This was simply an easier and more foolproof means to achieve the same end. According to the charging documents, the felony murder was predicated on felonious aggravated assault, which occurred when the McMichaels illegally followed and confronted Arbery with guns.

A very similar situation took place in response to the death of George Floyd while he was in police custody in Minneapolis, Minnesota. Officer Derek Chauvin, captured on video pressing his knee on Floyd's neck for over eight minutes, was charged with felony murder (categorized in Minnesota as second-degree murder) predicated on aggravated assault. As with the Arbery case, proving the requisite intent for conventional murder would be harder than you might think— or, at least riskier. Right or wrong, the defense attorney at trial would vigorously argue that the actual intention of Chauvin was to restrain Floyd, not to kill him. Guilty verdicts in criminal trials must always be unanimous. Thus, in order for "regular" murder charges to stick, all twelve Minnesota jurors would have to believe beyond a reasonable doubt that Chauvin intended to kill Floyd, and all twelve Georgia jurors would have to believe beyond a reasonable doubt that the McMichaels intended to kill Arbery. It only takes one insufficiently persuaded juror for a conviction to fail. If you were the prosecutor, wouldn't you go with the proverbial "sure bet" and charge felony murder instead?

Thus, a strange role-reversal has surfaced: the felony murder doctrine that has typically been derided by progressive thinkers as racially oppressive and unjust has recently formed the most tenable basis for charging and prosecuting the killers of two unarmed Black men for murder.

Has your initial reaction to the felony murder doctrine changed?

CRASH COURSE

Prosecutorial Power and Discretion

Here's a hot take for you: prosecutors are the most powerful people in the law. Okay, maybe it's not *that* hot; it's definitely been said before. For example, in 1940, Attorney General Robert Jackson famously proclaimed that "the prosecutor has more control over life, liberty, and reputation than any other person in America."

In the American criminal law system, prosecutors wield immense power, mostly due to the incredible amount of discretion afforded to them. Although their powers can vary slightly by jurisdiction, prosecutors generally decide whether or not to bring criminal charges, which charges to file, and when to offer plea bargains. Each of these prosecutorial actions have profound ramifications for defendants. And yet, prosecutors undertake these actions with nearly unreviewable discretion. Unlike many European and Latin American countries that require prosecutors to bring criminal charges for any case that is supported by reasonable evidence, the American criminal system enforces no such mandate. Prosecutors can decline to bring cases for just about any reason, including high workloads. In such situations, the offender is completely off the hook. Courts are very hesitant to intervene in a prosecutor's decision at any point in a case, and their conduct is simply assumed to be ethical. To be sure, many professions in the legal system are entrusted with discretion: police have discretion in enforcing laws, judges have discretion in presiding over trials, and parole boards have discretion in granting releases from prison. But no other profession enjoys such unchecked and sacred autonomy as the prosecutor.

With such discretion, concerns of abuse come naturally. While risks of political preference, nepotism, and other forms of favoritism raise serious concerns, accusations of racial bias (whether implicit or explicit) are most prevalent. Indeed, some surveys of prosecutorial records have shown that Black defendants have fewer cases dropped than white defendants, and also have their charges reduced in severity (e.g., from felony to misdemeanor) less frequently. As a real-world example, consider again the case of Ahmaud Arbery. Originally, after conducting an investigation into Arbery's death, which included viewing the video of Arbery's killing, the prosecutor (a white man from a rural, conservative county) declined to bring charges against the McMichaels. The case had completely stalled until the video footage of Arbery's death was released to the public more than two months after the killing, prompting national outrage and an investigation by the Georgia Bureau of Investigation. Just two days after the video went viral, the McMichaels were arrested and charged with felony murder by a different prosecutor. Had the video not found its way to the internet, it's very likely that no charges would have ever been filed, and such inaction would have simply fallen under the broad umbrella of prosecutorial discretion. The Attorney General of Georgia ultimately appointed a new prosecutor (a Black woman) from a different district to handle the case.

Although prosecutorial discretion has its faults, it can also serve some important functions. Proponents of prosecutorial discretion tend to support it for two main reasons. First, American criminal court dockets are notoriously backlogged and congested. There are simply far more prosecutable crimes than there are available working hours for prosecutors, judges, and juries. Prosecutors use their discretion to sift through a barrage of cases and efficiently select those that warrant the full services of our tax-funded judicial system. For the vast majority of criminal cases, prosecutors actually use their discretion to offer plea bargains to defendants, in which a defendant pleads guilty to a lesser charge in exchange for a more lenient sentence. For example, suppose a defendant was apprehended by police for breaking into a home and initially charged with burglary. Prior to trial, the prosecutor might offer a deal to the defendant to plead guilty to the lesser crime of trespassing in exchange for the burglary charge to be dropped. Proponents of plea bargaining argue that it is the most expedient and efficient way to keep the justice system functional and moving forward. It is estimated that around 95 percent of all cases in the United States are plea-bargained and never go to trial.

Second, many argue that a system of black-and-white rules cannot fully capture justice. Sound familiar? Indeed, sometimes true justice can be grey. Imagine that a state law makes it a felony to bring a weapon, including knives, onto school property. Seeking to deter violence at schools, the law imposes strict liability and allows for no exceptions. Imagine further that, today, a third grader has a birthday, for which her mother baked a cake to share with her class. Not thinking anything of it, the third grader puts a knife in her backpack in order to cut the cake. Her teacher discovers the knife and contacts the school administration, who then contact the police. Should this child be charged for violating the law? Most of us would say no, and would approve of a prosecutor using discretion to not charge this particular case. Examples such as this occur with great frequency each day throughout the country, with prosecutors declining to bring charges, even though the law has technically been broken. Should the husband who assists his terminally ill and suffering wife in committing suicide really face murder charges? Should the homeless woman who snuck into a local building to escape the winter cold really be charged with trespassing? Black-and-white laws often require a human element in order to enforce them in ways that comport with our sense of fairness and justice. This is where prosecutorial discretion can have its most significant benefit.

Marijuana Is Both Legal and Illegal
The Controlled Substance Act and Federal Preemption

It's a calm, quiet, and balmy summer afternoon. You're the proud owner of a new marijuana dispensary. Last year, your state passed sweeping legislation completely legalizing marijuana. While it was previously only allowed for medical purposes, it has since been fully legalized and permitted even for recreational use.

Always a keen entrepreneur, you jumped into the burgeoning market and opened up your shop. And what a success it has been! Sales are through the roof. Life is good. That is, until federal agents adorned in tactical gear burst through your front door, point guns at you and your customers, confiscate your products, and arrest you.

Stories similar to the one presented above have played out countless times across the country. A simple Google search for "federal agents raiding marijuana dispensary" will yield hundreds of news articles detailing nearly identical accounts in California, New Mexico, Colorado, Michigan, and elsewhere.

How is this happening? Why are marijuana shops that are operating legally being raided by federal authorities?

The legal issues surrounding these questions are fascinatingly complex and involve a stubborn clash between federal and state law, selective enforcement, and political pressures that span decades.

The Current Legal Landscape Surrounding Marijuana Laws

Let's begin by examining marijuana laws as they exist today—or, at least at the time of this book's writing. (The laws surrounding marijuana are ever-changing.)

California passed its infamous Proposition 215 in 1996, making the Golden State the very first to legalize marijuana for medicinal purposes. Following this, thirty-five more states, as well as the District of Columbia, passed similar laws allowing medical marijuana.

More recently, several states have gone a step further and fully legalized marijuana, allowing it for recreational purposes similar to the consumption of alcohol. However, even in such states, certain limitations exist limiting the amount of marijuana that can be possessed at one time and the amount that can legally be grown. Special licenses are also required to sell and profit off of marijuana.

As it stands today, marijuana is fully legal in fifteen states and the District of Columbia. Given the relatively large populations of some of these states (including California, Colorado, Illinois, Massachusetts, and New Jersey), around one hundred million people currently live in areas where marijuana is completely legal. Another twenty states have laws legalizing marijuana for medicinal purposes. Taken together, the overwhelming majority of our nation's population lives where marijuana is legally accessible in some form.

Or is it? Despite the rapidly increasing support for legalization at the state level, marijuana still remains illegal under federal law. In fact, as we will discover in a moment, the federal government treats marijuana as one of the most dangerous drugs on the planet.

Federal laws surrounding marijuana stem primarily from the Controlled Substance Act (CSA). The CSA is a comprehensive statute establishing the federal laws under which the manufacture, importation, possession, use, and distribution of most drugs is regulated and criminalized. If an individual is ever charged federally with a drug crime, it's very likely that the CSA is the law that has been violated. The CSA regulates most of the common drugs you've probably heard of, such as marijuana, methamphetamine, cocaine, LSD, heroin, ecstasy, oxycodone, steroids, codeine, and many more. However, not all drugs fall under the purview of the CSA—alcohol and tobacco are curiously exempt from its scope, an outcome that most attribute to successful political lobbying.

The CSA categorizes drugs hierarchically into one of five "Schedules" based on their potential for abuse and medical value. Schedule 1 drugs are viewed as the most dangerous, having the highest potential for abuse and lowest medical value, whereas those in Schedule 5 are considered the least dangerous. The higher a drug ranks in the scheduling hierarchy, the more restrictions and regulations apply. Bewildering to many, marijuana is classified as a Schedule 1 drug, in the same category as heroin. Perhaps even more shocking, cocaine and methamphetamine are listed one step below in Schedule 2.

Yes, the CSA actually classifies meth as less problematic than marijuana, despite the fact that thousands of people overdose from meth each year and effectively zero die from marijuana.

Among the legal community, the vast majority of scholars and commentators view marijuana's placement as a Schedule 1 drug as antiquated and unjustifiable. In addition to influencing criminal penalties, marijuana's status as a Schedule 1 drug means that conducting any scientific research involving the drug is highly restricted. Currently, the University of Mississippi is home to the only facility in the United States federally approved to grow marijuana for research purposes. Since the CSA's inception in 1970, activists have lobbied vigorously for marijuana to be rescheduled to a lower position, or removed from the CSA entirely (similar to alcohol and tobacco). However, each attempt has been met only with failure.

But . . . Why?

Proponents of categorizing marijuana as a Schedule 1 drug often argue that neuropsychological research shows marijuana can be addictive and harmful, particularly for developing adolescent brains. They also claim that insufficient evidence exists demonstrating marijuana's true medical value; specifically, that no controlled, large-scale clinical studies have yielded persuasive results or adequate safety protocols. However, pro-marijuana activists would disagree about the dearth of scientific evidence, pointing to several studies that demonstrate marijuana's efficacy in treating chronic pain and nausea induced from chemotherapy. Additionally, marijuana's categorization in Schedule 1 can be thought of as a fundamental Catch-22—it cannot be moved from Schedule 1 until more scientific evidence demonstrates its medical benefits, but the tight restrictions placed on its study as a Schedule 1 drug make this type of research nearly impossible to undertake.

The classification of marijuana in Schedule 1 can perhaps be best explained by the political dynamics at the time of the CSA's enactment. During the 1970s, many American politicians were obsessed over concerns that unfettered marijuana use would lead to grave societal ills. Racism no doubt underpinned some aspect of this concern, given that the majority of marijuana users at the time were Black and Hispanic. The political sensationalism around marijuana's purported ill effects can be readily seen in the testimony from Mississippi Senator James Eastland during a 1974 Senate hearing, where he derided recent student protests at University of California, Berkeley and warned, "If the cannabis epidemic continues to spread at the rate of the post-Berkeley period, we may find ourselves saddled with a large population of semi-zombies." Following the 1970s, the nation's drug philosophy shifted into nearly three decades of the "Just Say No" era, with D.A.R.E (Drug Abuse Resistance Education) programs proliferating throughout school systems from coast to coast and labeling marijuana a dangerous "gateway" drug. The position of marijuana as a Schedule 1 drug became firmly entrenched, and it has been immovable ever since.

CRASH COURSE

The Commerce Clause

Astute observers might be wondering why marijuana, even when possessed, manufactured, or distributed strictly inside a single state, is *federally* illegal. Recall from our previous discussions that federal laws must relate to some federal nexus. Typically, the requisite federal nexus is satisfied when actions cross state lines, occur on federal property, involve federal employees, or implicate national issues such as immigration, terrorism, or the economy. By explicit constitutional design, federal lawmakers (i.e., Congress) have some important limitations to their authority; they cannot gallivant around the nation enacting laws wherever they see fit.

Or can they?

Enter the Commerce Clause, or as many lawyers think of it, the law that allows the federal government to do pretty much whatever it wants. The Commerce Clause is found in Article 1 of the Constitution and grants Congress the power "to regulate commerce with foreign nations, and among the several states, and with the Indian Tribes." The key aspect for our discussion is the authority of Congress to regulate commerce "among the several states." As we will see, this single grant of power has led to enormous consequences—the CSA being one of them.

At the time of its drafting, the Commerce Clause was designed to ease trading conflicts among the thirteen colony states. Because each state initially operated essentially as its own sovereign entity, many states were erecting trade barriers to protect their own businesses from competing colonies. The assortment of inconsistent and complicated trading laws throughout the country resulted in a significant economic downturn nationwide. To address this issue, the Founding Fathers believed that the federal government was best suited to regulate the complexities of interstate commerce, rather than a patchwork of independent states. Thus, the Commerce Clause was included in the drafting of the Constitution.

Yet, as history unfolded, a series of Supreme Court rulings incrementally expanded the powers vested within the Commerce Clause. Eventually, Congress found themselves able to regulate an incredibly broad array of activities, even including those that take place squarely within a single state (i.e., intrastate activities). For example, in 1938, Congress passed the Fair Labor Standards Act ("FLSA") to regulate many aspects of employment, including minimum wages, overtime pay, and the use of child labor. Because a law regulating employment conditions had no ostensible relevance to interstate commerce, it was quickly challenged as being unconstitutional. The Supreme Court took up the issue in United States v. Darby and surprised many by finding the law to be a valid exercise of Commerce Clause authority. Specifically, the Court reasoned that the law prevented states from using substandard labor practices to gain an economic advantage in interstate commerce. Put another way, if one state, say, Oklahoma, had little to no employee protections, an Oklahoma business could outcompete a business from another state—say, Arkansas—that did offer employees benefits like overtime pay and minimum wages. The great length to which the Court stretched the Commerce Clause green-lit Congress to enact numerous broad-sweeping federal laws, with many—including the FLSA—still existing today.

Incredibly, from the 1930s to the 1990s, no federal law was invalidated by the Supreme Court on the basis of exceeding Commerce Clause authority. It was not until 1995, in the case of United States v. Lopez, that the Supreme Court finally initiated a minor halt on the continued expansion of federal law. In Lopez, a defendant had been charged with carrying a handgun to school in violation of the federal Gun Free School Zones Act, which (as the name suggests) prohibited knowingly bringing a firearm onto a school zone. The defendant argued that the federal government had no authority to regulate firearms in local schools. Lawyers for the government countered that the law fell under the authority of the Commerce Clause because the possession of a firearm in a school zone would lead to violent crime, which would in turn affect general economic conditions throughout the country. Although the Supreme Court had swallowed a lot of questionable government arguments over the prior decades, this one was finally a bridge too far. The Court struck down the law as unconstitutional, explaining plainly that it "neither regulates a commercial activity nor contains a requirement that the possession [of a firearm] be connected in any way to interstate commerce."

In a fascinating display of legislative obstinance, Congress reacted to the Supreme Court's decision in Lopez by promptly rewriting the Gun Free School Zones Act to include the necessary interstate commerce "hook." The law still exists today and now reads: "It shall be unlawful for any individual knowingly to possess a firearm that has moved in or that otherwise affects interstate or foreign commerce at a place that the individual knows . . . is a school zone." The new version of the law has yet to be examined by the Supreme Court, and many legal scholars are anxiously waiting to see if the mere inclusion of the buzzwords "interstate" and "commerce," without any other substantive change, suffices to make it constitutional.

Returning to the topic of marijuana, the Supreme Court heard the case of Gonzales v. Raich in 2005, which challenged the constitutionality of the CSA. Departing from the stricter view in Lopez, the Court upheld the validity of the CSA, explaining that the Commerce Clause allows Congress to regulate purely local activities (such as the possession of marijuana) so long as they have a substantial effect on the national economy. Unlike the Gun Free School Zones Act, the CSA does involve, at least tangentially, economic activities throughout the country. As explained by the Court, the local use of marijuana affects supply and demand in the national marijuana marketplace, thereby affecting interstate commerce.

Do you find these rationales from the Supreme Court convincing? If not, you are far from alone. As explained by many legal scholars, the Supreme Court's expansive view of the Commerce Clause likely stems from the belief that a strong federal government is needed to help shepherd a rapidly evolving nation. Consider, for example, the case of <u>United States v. Darby</u>, which upheld the validity of the FLSA. It is perhaps justifiable to believe that the federal government is best suited to regulate important areas of life such as working conditions, and that these regulations should apply uniformly across the nation for the benefit of all citizens. Yet, Congress can only make laws using the powers vested to it in the Constitution—the most broad and malleable being the Commerce Clause. By greatly expanding their interpretation of the Commerce Clause, the Supreme Court was able to uphold the federal regulation they desired, while still (at least in theory) abiding by the rules of the Constitution.

Preemption and the Supremacy Clause

With <u>Gonzales v. Raich</u> having established that the CSA is valid federal law, the next question to address is why state laws that seem to blatantly contradict it are allowed to exist.

The Supremacy Clause of the Constitution declares that federal law "shall be the supreme Law of the Land." Indeed, you may have heard before that federal law always trumps state law. This is generally true, with all federal statutes, regulations, and treaties standing in an elevated position of authority above any state law. Under the doctrine of federal preemption, if a state law ever "conflicts" with a federal law, the state law must be preempted by the federal law (i.e., the federal law must prevail).

At first glance, and perhaps even after a second or third, it would appear that state laws legalizing marijuana create a clear conflict with the CSA prohibiting it. However, courts have not viewed these sets of laws as creating the kind of legal conflict that necessitates preemption. The logic behind this surprising perspective is based on two main rationales.

First, the law has historically shied away from federal preemption when it comes to states exercising their "police powers." As we have previously discussed, the Tenth Amendment gives state governments the power to police their jurisdiction and enact criminal laws suited to their specific population. Courts have generally accepted the notion that states know how to police their citizenry themselves.

Second, a provision of the CSA, Section 903, explicitly states that Congress did not intend for federal law to preempt state law "unless there is a positive conflict between [the CSA] and . . . State law so that the two cannot consistently stand together." This sets a very high bar for federal preemption. As explained in <u>County of San Diego v. San Diego NORML</u>, a state marijuana law will only be preempted if it is "physically impossible" to comply with both the state law and the CSA. Under this "impossibility preemption" standard, a state law would have to actually require someone to violate the CSA for it to be invalidated. Of course, no state marijuana law mandates that citizens possess, distribute, or manufacture marijuana; they simply allow them to do so. Congress may have included this important language in Section 903 for a variety of reasons. For example, they may not have wanted to undertake the full burden of enacting drug laws. Or, perhaps they wished to pay deference to the Tenth Amendment police powers allotted to states. Records of the deliberations in Congress while drafting Section 903 are limited, so we don't know for sure.

Federal Penalties for Marijuana Crimes Under the CSA

As a Schedule 1 drug, federal penalties for marijuana can be significant. Getting caught in possession of any amount of marijuana can lead to a prison sentence of up to one year. If charged with distributing or manufacturing marijuana, the penalties increase substantially. For example, selling marijuana in any quantity carries a potential five-year prison sentence. Cultivating more than fifty marijuana plants can result in a whopping twenty-year maximum sentence. While growing more than fifty plants might seem excessive for the average person, consider the marijuana dispensaries that grow their own products, or the commercial growing operations that supply the thousands of dispensaries throughout the country. Many states explicitly offer cultivation licenses allowing businesses to grow hundreds and even thousands of plants at a time. In other words, an individual could be growing fifty marijuana plants for their dispensary in full compliance with state law, but still be subject to twenty years in prison under federal law. As bizarre as this might all seem, the clash between federal and state law has certainly had real-world effects for some unlucky individuals.

In Michigan, one former owner of a marijuana dispensary, Danny Trevino, was recently sentenced to fifteen years in prison. Federal authorities charged him with a litany of crimes, including manufacturing, distributing, and possessing large quantities of marijuana. Although Trevino vigorously maintained that his actions were legal under state law, the judge in the case, Judge Paul Maloney, stuck firm to the federal law on the books. "I fully recognize that the landscape has changed in many states in this country," Maloney reportedly explained, "[but the] fact is, marijuana is a Schedule 1 controlled substance."

While Judge Maloney handed down a hefty punishment to Trevino, it's important to note that the general trend over the last few years has been to move away from severe prison sentences for marijuana offenses. In the United States, at both the federal and state level, it is the role of the judge to make punishment determinations (i.e., decide how long a defendant should stay in prison, or if probation or fines are more appropriate in lieu of jail time). While many crimes have established minimum and maximum punishment requirements, or suggested sentencing guidelines to follow, judges have significant discretion to operate within these bounds as they see fit.

Pursuant to the CSA, a defendant found guilty of possessing any Schedule 1 drug faces a maximum prison sentence of one year, and a minimum fine of one thousand dollars. As we have discussed, marijuana and heroin are both Schedule 1 drugs. In all likelihood, however, a judge will sentence a defendant found guilty of marijuana possession more leniently than a defendant found guilty of heroin possession. Many judges might not require any prison time at all for the marijuana offender, and instead impose only the fine of one thousand dollars as mandated by law. By contrast, most judges will require the heroin offender to face some amount of jail time. Indeed, annual reports from the United States Sentencing Commission clearly demonstrate that marijuana offenders face significantly less prison time than comparable heroin offenders.

Given the significant discretion afforded to judges during sentencing, prison sentences often trend with society's prevailing view of certain crimes. As a deadly heroin epidemic sweeps through the United States at the same time that marijuana is becoming more widely accepted, there is no doubt that judges will tend to punish marijuana crimes less severely than heroin offenses, even if the law doesn't explicitly treat them any differently.

To Enforce or Not to Enforce

We have already discussed at length the concept of prosecutorial discretion. Perhaps nowhere else is this discretion more apparent than in the federal government's mercurial enforcement of marijuana crimes. Ever since California first legalized medical marijuana in the 1990s, the federal government has struggled to guide its prosecutors on when and where to actually enforce the CSA's marijuana laws. After all, federal resources are limited, and many believe that these precious resources should not be devoted to prosecuting those who are acting in compliance with their own state's laws.

When tricky issues of federal law are at play, the Attorney General (appointed by the president to be the head of the Department of Justice and responsible for enforcing federal law), will often send a guidance memorandum to all federal prosecutors working under his or her authority. As stated in various memos during the presidential administrations of Bill Clinton and George Bush, prosecutors were encouraged to prosecute all marijuana crimes, irrespective of their status under state law. However, under President Barack Obama, the Department of Justice changed course and issued a new memo in 2009 encouraging prosecutors not to bring charges against those who possess or distribute marijuana in accordance with the laws of their state. In 2013, another Obama-era memo further encouraged prosecutors not to enforce federal marijuana laws unless a defendant's actions fell within a series of "enforcement principles," such as selling marijuana to minors, using marijuana proceeds to fund gang activities, or using weapons during the purchase or distribution of marijuana.

Things changed once again as President Trump came into power. During Trump's tenure, his Department of Justice rescinded all of the Obama-era memos and instead issued its own, directing prosecutors to simply "weigh all relevant considerations" when making prosecuting decisions. In response to the recission of the Obama memos, many feared that federal prosecutors might engage in a new "War on Drugs" to combat rising marijuana use throughout the country. However, a review of the records from federal prosecutions during the Trump administration revealed that prosecutors largely ignored the recission of the Obama-era memos and continued to stick to the same enforcement principles set out in the 2013 memo. An important point to note is that federal prosecutors, like most federal employees, are career employees who perform their duties through multiple presidential administrations and fluctuating political climates. A new administration does not necessarily bring with it a complete overhaul of an entire federal system (and most believe that it shouldn't). Today, federal prosecutions for marijuana offenses remain relatively infrequent compared to other drug crimes, particularly where state law has legalized the drug. Technically, federal authorities can prosecute individuals for marijuana crimes, even in states where it is completely legal, but this rarely ever takes place. More likely, federal prosecutors will use their discretion and turn a blind eye to violations in such states.

The Government Can Take Your Stuff without Ever Charging You with a Crime
Civil Forfeiture

United States v. Approximately 64,695 Pounds of Shark Fins

Check out the name of this case. Yes, it's real. So what's going on here?

First, let's clarify a few things. When citing legal cases, the two names listed are the parties involved in the dispute. In civil lawsuits, case names will look like Miller v. Williams or Garcia v. Walmart. In criminal cases, the governing body responsible for bringing the criminal charges forms one party, and the defendant is the other. State criminal case names look something like State of California v. Smith or Commonwealth of Massachusetts v. Johnson (often abbreviated to simply State v. Smith and Commonwealth v. Johnson). In federal criminal cases, the entire United States technically forms the governing body bringing charges, so case names look like United States v. Boehner. The entity bringing the lawsuit or criminal charges is the first name listed, and the entity being sued or being charged with a crime is the second name.

Often, there are more than two parties to a legal action. For example, Bob Jones and his friend, John Springfield, got into a car accident caused by faulty brakes in Bob's Ford vehicle. Bob and John both want to sue not only Ford, but also the brake manufacturer and the service shop that had recently inspected the vehicle and failed to notice the defect. Instead of a clunky case name such as <u>Jones and Springfield v. Ford, Brake Manufacturer, and Service Shop</u>, the case name will simply include the parties on each side of the dispute that are listed first in the court documents—e.g., <u>Jones v. Ford</u>.

Now that we've gotten that all buttoned up, let's look again at that weird case name, <u>United States v. Approximately 64,695 Pounds of Shark Fins</u>.

According to what we just learned, the federal government is instituting some kind of case against . . . "approximately 64,695 pounds of shark fins?" That's right! In this case, the federal government is actually suing the shark fins in order to take possession of them—a legal process termed "civil forfeiture."

Civil forfeiture allows police to seize property that they have probable cause to believe is involved in criminal activity. Once the property is seized, a civil lawsuit *against that property* is initiated by the government in order to take possession of it (i.e., the owner of the property is compelled by a court to forfeit their right to it).

While it's actually not uncommon for non-human entities to be subject to lawsuits (for example, business entities and other kinds of institutions are sued all the time), seldom are *tangible things* parties to a lawsuit. Civil forfeiture is thus highly unique and often results in totally absurd case names, such as <u>United States v. Forty Barrels and Twenty Kegs of Coca-Cola</u>, <u>Texas v. One Gold Crucifix</u>, and <u>United States v. Article Consisting of 50,000 Cardboard Boxes More or Less, Each Containing One Pair of Clacker Balls</u>.

To examine how the civil forfeiture process actually works, let's review the famous case of <u>United States v. $63,530.00 in U.S. Currency</u>. In 2011, Douglas County Sheriff's Deputy Dave Wintle initiated a traffic stop of Mark Brewer after observing him as he crossed three lanes of traffic on a Nebraska interstate without signaling. While Deputy Wintle ran a criminal background check from Brewer's license and registration, he chatted with Brewer about his activities that day. Brewer explained that he was traveling to Los Angeles to visit his uncle and find employment. He further explained that he was thinking about purchasing a house in California.

Deputy Wintle's record check revealed no criminal history, and he informed Brewer that he would not be issuing him a citation for the illegal lane changes. Before he departed, however, Deputy Wintle asked a few more questions about the contents of Brewer's vehicle, including whether or not he possessed any weapons, drugs, or large amounts of cash. Brewer answered no to each question. Deputy Wintle then asked Brewer if he could run a drug-sniffing dog around the perimeter of the vehicle. Remember, Illinois v. Caballes ruled that the police can use drug dogs without any probable cause or consent, but only if the traffic stop is not delayed beyond a normal timeframe. Deputy Wintle had already told Brewer that he would not be issuing him a traffic citation; thus, the normal timeframe of the traffic stop had concluded. In order to use the drug dog, Deputy Wintle needed either a reasonable suspicion of contraband inside the vehicle (which he didn't have) or Brewer's consent. Unfortunately for Brewer, he consented. The dog ended up alerting to the driver's side of the vehicle and the trunk.

Now with probable cause to fully search the vehicle, Deputy Wintle found a backpack in the trunk. Upon opening the backpack, Deputy Wintle allegedly noticed a very strong odor of marijuana. Inside the backpack, he found sixty-four bundles of cash wrapped in plastic bags, totaling $63,530. Deputy Wintle questioned Brewer about the large amount of money and Brewer explained that it was intended for a down payment on a house. No drugs were ultimately found inside the backpack or car, but Deputy Wintle did uncover two articles titled "How to Make Wicked Hash" and "How to Make Weed Oil without Blowing Yourself Up." Believing that the money was associated with illegal drug activity, Deputy Wintle seized it and sent Brewer on his way, without charging him with any crime or even writing him a ticket.

Several months later, the government filed a lawsuit against the $63,530, seeking forfeiture. Brewer attempted to fight the forfeiture, arguing that the government had failed to demonstrate a sufficient connection between the seized money and any drug activity. Brewer maintained that the money was intended for a down payment on a house. Nevertheless, the court disagreed with Brewer and found that the government had offered enough evidence to show that the money was associated with drug activity. In particular, the court pointed to Brewer's initial dishonest answer to Deputy Wintle's question about possessing large amounts of currency, the hidden nature of the money wrapped in plastic and in a backpack in the trunk of the car, the strong smell of marijuana emanating from the backpack, the drug-sniffing dog's alert to the car, and the articles relating to marijuana manufacturing found in

Brewer's possession. Thus, although Brewer was never charged with any drug crimes, and although the government did not definitively prove that the money was related to drug activity, he lost his $63,530.

It's important here to note that civil forfeiture operates under civil law, which is a distinct set of laws from criminal law. In fact, the distinctions between civil and criminal law are so important, we should jump into a quick CRASH COURSE to talk about them.

CRASH COURSE

Criminal Law vs. Civil Law

In the American legal system, both criminal and civil laws address wrongdoing. Criminal laws generally govern behaviors that are considered offenses against the public. Even offenses against an individual person can still be considered "public" because such actions ultimately harm society as a whole. Overall, criminal laws exist to keep order and protect the public from harm. Violations of criminal laws are prosecuted by the government, and the prosecutor (not the victim) files the charges in court as a representative of the government. Classic examples of criminal laws are things like murder, arson, burglary, drunk driving, and, as we have now discussed in detail, drug possession, manufacturing, and distribution.

By contrast, civil law governs disputes between individuals or institutions regarding the legal duties and responsibilities they owe to one another. Civil laws often control the more private spheres of life, such as one's contractual rights, property, employment, or marriage. When civil law has been violated, the aggrieved party files the case themselves. Examples of civil law violations include breaches of contract, employment discrimination, improper evictions by a landlord, and conduct causing personal injury or property damage (also referred to as "torts"—more on this later).

While the differences between criminal and civil law can be articulated in broad umbrella terms, the reality is that both bodies of law often blend together in practice. For example, most states have both criminal and civil laws against sexual assault. The act of stealing can likewise be both a crime and a civil wrong. Even the death of a person can be both a crime (murder) and a civil violation (wrongful death). Indeed, there are innumerable instances in which criminal and civil law overlap.

Perhaps, then, it is best to differentiate criminal versus civil laws by the types of punishment violators of each will incur. Violators of criminal law face punishment imposed by the government, which typically includes imprisonment. Violators of civil law are most often forced by a court to pay money to the party they have wronged. Other times, civil courts can simply order these violators to do something (e.g., make good on a contract) or stop doing something (e.g., cease infringement on a copyright).

Criminal Trials vs. Civil Trials

Alleged violations of criminal and civil law are both ultimately adjudicated in trials. There are numerous differences between criminal and civil trials, many of which are quite complicated and frankly boring. For the purposes of this book, you only need to know two things:

First, it is much easier to meet the evidentiary burden (i.e., provide sufficient evidence) to win a civil lawsuit than it is to meet the evidentiary burden to find someone guilty of a crime. To get a bit technical, a prosecutor must prove "beyond a reasonable doubt" that a defendant committed a crime. Although courts do not attach or assign numerical values to the standard, legal scholars often think of it as requiring a certainty of around 99 percent. The relative difficulty of proving a criminal case can be summarized by a popular legal adage: "Is my client guilty? Probably! But probably isn't good enough!"

By contrast, civil cases require proof by "the preponderance of the evidence." This standard has been thought of as requiring only 51 percent certainty. Basically, an aggrieved party in a civil suit must only show that it is more likely than not that the offender violated the law. This is a drastically lower standard compared to criminal trials. To further illustrate this point, consider the murders of Nicole Brown Simpson and Ronald Goldman, "allegedly" committed by O.J. Simpson. (The word allegedly is placed in quotations because, in 2007, Simpson co-wrote a book, *If I Did It: Confessions of the Killer*, which puts forth the hypothetical description of how he murdered Nicole Brown Simpson and Ronald Goldman. Notably, on the book's cover art, the word "If" was intentionally written in a tiny font to make it just barely legible. You can make your own decisions here.) Despite being found not guilty in criminal court, a civil trial found O.J. Simpson liable for the deaths. This is because the evidentiary burden in his criminal case was much higher than it was in the civil case against him.

Second, many essential Constitutional protections do not apply in civil trials. For example, a defendant in a criminal case is always entitled to an attorney, and if they can't afford one, the state must provide one. In contrast, parties in a civil case don't have the right to an attorney, so if they can't afford one, they'll have to represent themselves (which almost always ends poorly). Many other protections, such as the Fifth Amendment's protection against self-incrimination (you cannot be compelled to testify against yourself) only apply to criminal trials.

Returning to the case of Brewer's $63,530: because the forfeiture was pursued under civil law, the government only needed to show by a preponderance of the evidence (i.e., 51 percent certainty) that the money was associated with drug activity. Due to this relatively low standard of proof, the court found in favor of the government. By contrast, if Brewer were facing actual criminal charges for some kind of drug offense related to the money, the circumstantial evidence offered by police would have never been sufficient to find him guilty beyond a reasonable doubt (i.e., 99 percent certainty).

Opponents of civil forfeiture argue that the practice is particularly insidious because the government can utilize the "easier" civil system to achieve punishments more akin to criminal law. Some states don't even try to hide these punitive goals. For example, in Texas, the civil forfeiture law actually lies within the state's code of criminal laws, as opposed to its code of civil laws.

Police Funding and The Equitable Sharing Loophole

Okay, still sticking with the $63,530 that Brewer lost. *Sucks for him—but where did it go?* Buckle up, because what follows is a real doozy.

In many (if not most) civil forfeiture cases, the forfeited property ultimately goes to the police department that seized it. As the practice of civil forfeiture has become more frequent, more than half of all police departments now explicitly depend on forfeiture revenues in order to fund equipment, salaries, and bonuses. In some states, civil forfeitures fund nearly 40 percent of police budgets. With very little in the way of accountability regarding the expenditure of these funds, many have reported forfeited funds being spent on extravagancies like fancy dinners and parties for police personnel. In the small town of New Braunfels, Texas, police outfitted a one thousand-horsepower Corvette Z06 as a patrol vehicle after seizing it as part of a drug raid. According to many commentators, the civil forfeiture paradigm creates a perverse incentive for police to seize property from citizens. A concern exists that the decision to pursue a forfeiture is governed not by justice, but rather by police wish lists.

In recent years, lawmakers in many states have started to question the relationship between civil forfeiture and law enforcement, and have worked to reform existing practices. More than a dozen states now require a criminal conviction before pursuing civil forfeiture. A few have outlawed the practice entirely. At the same time, other states have passed laws requiring proceeds of forfeiture to be put into the state's general fund, rather than going directly to police departments. Missouri has passed particularly strong reforms, not only requiring a criminal conviction prior to civil forfeiture, but also mandating that all forfeited funds be directed to public schools.

Sound promising? Not so fast! Enter the federal government's Equitable Sharing Program. Even in states that have passed robust reforms, the Equitable Sharing Program offers a powerful federal work-around, allowing police to still retain the lion's share of forfeited funds. Here's how it works: local or state police seize property that they believe is associated with criminal activity. If the alleged criminal activity also violates federal law, police simply hand over the seized property to the federal government to pursue the civil asset forfeiture. As we have discussed, the federal government has crafty ways of finding jurisdiction even where it does not overtly exist. Most commonly in forfeiture cases, federal jurisdiction is triggered when the alleged contraband property has crossed state lines. If the federal government wins the case (which they most often do), 80 percent of the proceeds are returned to the original police department that made the seizure. Think of this return of funds as a nice little thank you for their "sharing" with the federal government. Overall, even if state law has put limits on questionable civil forfeiture practices, the federal loophole can circumvent those restrictions.

Returning one final time to Brewer and his forfeited $63,530, those of you with a particularly keen eye may have noticed something peculiar about the case name: **United States v. $63,530.00 in U.S. Currency**. According to the facts of the case that we discussed, Brewer was pulled over by a county sheriff's deputy in Nebraska. After learning about the facts of the case, you may have initially wondered: *Why isn't the case titled* **The State of Nebraska v. $63,530.00 in U.S. Currency**? Equitable sharing is the answer! The case is titled United States v. $63,530.00 in U.S. Currency, rather than The State of Nebraska v. $63,530.00 in U.S. Currency, precisely because the federal government had assumed control of the case via equitable sharing.

For now, the Equitable Sharing Program is alive and well, with billions of dollars' worth of forfeited property flowing into federal coffers each year. Remember Missouri's robust civil forfeiture reforms? Recent reports demonstrated that of the $19,000,000 collected in civil forfeitures in Missouri over the last three years, only $340,000 has gone to schools. The rest was routed back to police departments via equitable sharing.

But . . . Why?

In spite of all the problematic practices we have covered thus far, civil forfeiture laws actually have positive intentions at heart. When used for their proper purpose, these laws have historically enjoyed bipartisan support.

Proponents of civil forfeitures contend that the practice is an effective tool in the overall law enforcement repertoire. Civil forfeitures have routinely been used to target vehicles, real estate, and other valuables owned by drug kingpins and mobsters, as well as money from Wall Street con artists. In fact, civil forfeiture laws helped the government seize funds that Bernie Madoff had swindled in his infamous Ponzi scheme.

Civil forfeitures have been given particular praise as a powerful weapon to curb the flow of foreign drug money into the United States. Although the tactics have been criticized as racially discriminatory, many police departments located near the Mexican border are specially trained to identify suspected drug traffickers and seize their property. Law enforcement officials often claim that civil forfeitures are among the most effective tactics to hamper drug smuggling activities. One sheriff in Texas went so far as to proclaim that Mexican cartels will build monuments to honor any American lawmakers who abolish civil forfeiture.

In some cases that involve international criminals, civil forfeiture is actually the only way to confiscate the instrumentalities of crime. Imagine a Chinese spy ring has infiltrated the United States. In order to fund their espionage, several secret bank accounts have been opened throughout the country, with large sums of money being deposited every month. The FBI catches wind of the spy ring and immediately seizes the bank accounts, but the spies are able to flee back to China before being apprehended by law enforcement. Because China has no extradition agreement with the United States, these spies will never be prosecuted for any crimes. Civil forfeiture would be the only way to confiscate the funds in the bank accounts and achieve some measure of justice.

Overall, proponents of civil forfeiture argue that such laws are too critical of a law enforcement practice to abolish, and that improper seizures are statistically rare. Opponents contend that civil forfeiture motivates police abuse and fundamentally violates constitutional principles by imposing criminal-type punishment under the guise of civil law. And yet, many simply sit somewhere in the middle of the controversy, believing in the utility of civil forfeiture as a practice, but also supporting the elimination of the Equitable Sharing Program so that states can impose more regulations on the practice.

SECTION 3: SELF-DEFENSE

You Have to Be Really Scared Before You Can Legally Shoot Someone
The Reasonable Person Standard

At their core, self-defense laws were created to support the rational notion that you have a right to protect yourself from harm. While the idea of self-defense might conjure up thoughts of the Wild West, these laws have only recently expanded within the last few decades to become quite broad. Before jumping straight into the legality of shooting people, let's begin by discussing the basic principles of self-defense. Today, the specifics of these laws vary throughout each state, but generally speaking, self-defense is warranted if your actions satisfy each of the following four categories:

(1) Imminent Danger: Self-defense must be in response to an imminent threat of harm, meaning that the harm is happening *now*, in this very moment. Danger that is perceived to be an issue in the near future or at some other point in time will not be considered imminent. For example, if someone threatens you by saying, "Watch your back tomorrow! I'm going to get you!" it's still too early to use self-defense.

(2) Provocation: Self-defense cannot be used if you initiated the confrontation that gave rise to the imminent threat of harm. This should make logical sense. It would be absurd to allow someone to pick a fight and then claim self-defense as their opponent fought back. That said, there are two exceptions to this rule. You can provoke the confrontation and still use self-defense if (1) the other person responds with excessive force under the circumstances and significantly escalates the situation, or (2) you withdraw from the initial provocation and the other person persists. For example, if Sam pushes Kris and Kris pulls out a knife (responding with excessive force), Sam can defend himself from the knife attack and still claim self-defense. Additionally, if Sam pushes Kris but then walks away with his hands in the air saying, "Never mind, I don't want to fight you!" but Kris follows Sam and punches him anyways, Sam can also defend himself. The specific facts and contexts of self-defense claims are always extremely important to analyze.

(3) **Proportionate Force:** the degree of force used to protect your-self must be proportional to the danger you face. For example, if some-one flicks your buttocks with a towel, you cannot respond by breaking their jaw.

(4) **Reasonable Belief:** Your belief that harm was imminent, and that self-defense was necessary in order to avoid that harm, must be "reasonable." This reasonableness standard is usually what decides all self-defense claims, and it's importance cannot be understated. But what exactly is a reasonable belief? Welcome again to the wonderfully grey world of the law!

Here's where the importance of juries comes into play. Whether or not a belief is reasonable is traditionally decided by a jury. More often than not, a juror will be asked to place themselves in the same situation and ask, "What would I have done?" In theory, one of the main purposes of the jury is to act as the ultimate assessor of reasonableness. Indeed, a jury is supposed to be a cross-section of the community chosen at random. Who better to decide what is reasonable than a group of supposedly reasonable people? (More on the realities of jury selection later on.)

While this "reasonable person" construct lies at the crux of self-defense laws, it also plays a critical role in numerous other areas of the law, from criminal law to contract law. The imaginary reasonable person made his first appearance in the 1837 case of Vaughan v. Menlove. Menlove had stacked hay on his property in a manner that was prone to spontaneous ignition. (Yes, hay is very flammable, apparently.) After being warned repeatedly that his hay posed a fire hazard, Menlove simply responded that he would "chance it." Unfortunately for Menlove, the hay eventually did ignite and caused a fire that burned down his own barn and stable before spreading to near-by cottages owned by Vaughan. Vaughan sued Menlove in civil court for the damage he suffered from his destroyed property. During trial, Menlove's lawyer admitted to his client's "misfortune of not possessing the highest order of intelligence." In other words, he called him super dumb. The lawyer attempted to argue that Menlove should not be found guilty if he acted within his *own* best judgment, even if that judgment wasn't particularly prudent. However, the court disagreed and instead ruled that Menlove's conduct should be compared against the objective standard of the "reasonable person."

As applied to cases of self-defense, if you possess an irrational phobia of people with red hair and react to a random ginger-haired fellow walking past you on the street by attacking him in a fit of terror, your bizarre and subjective sense of fear will not give you the legal right to defend yourself; a reasonable person in your same situation must also find that self-defense was necessary.

Deadly Force in Self-Defense

Okay, now that we understand the basics, it's time for the pièce de resistance: using deadly force in self-defense. The first thing to understand is that no one actually needs to die for force to be considered "deadly." Deadly force is simply force that is reasonably capable of causing someone to die; death need not occur. For example, imagine you are being attacked by an assailant and you shoot at them with your gun. Despite months of training at the range, you are still a dreadful shot. Even though your bullet completely misses the assailant, you have still used deadly force, because all gun shots are reasonably capable of causing death.

The legal standard for the use of deadly force in self-defense is actually extremely similar to the general self-defense analysis we already discussed. The only difference is the extent of the harm that you reasonably believe is imminent. To use deadly force, you must reasonably believe that you are facing an imminent threat of great bodily harm or death. Based on our previous discussion of proportionality, this should come as no surprise. If the level of defensive force used must be proportional to the imminent threat faced, using deadly force necessitates that some very serious harm is being threatened.

Across all states, the "reasonable belief of an imminent threat of great bodily harm or death" is by far the most common standard for permitting deadly force, so let's refer to this as the "general standard." Although the general standard applies in the majority of states, we mustn't forget that places like Florida and Texas also exist! Indeed, a handful of states permit deadly force in a few other situations—some of them quite surprising.

Under Florida law, there are two distinct routes to justify the use of deadly force. The first route is the "general standard." However, Florida also permits deadly force in order to prevent the imminent commission of a "forcible felony." Florida law categorizes numerous crimes as forcible felonies, including treason, murder, sexual battery, carjacking, robbery, burglary, arson, aggravated assault, and aggravated stalking. Technically, under Florida law, you could witness a carjacking as it's taking place and legally use deadly force to prevent the commission of that crime. You could also theoretically witness an individual attempt to set fire to a home and use deadly force against that person in order to prevent the arson.

In Texas, things are even more extreme. True to its motto, everything is bigger in Texas, including the legal ability to use deadly force. Texas is the only state in the nation that permits deadly force to protect property. Under Texas law, deadly force is permitted if it is necessary to stop the commission of a theft, or to stop a thief from fleeing with property—but only at nighttime. That's right, the ability to use deadly force is dependent on the time of day. Specifically, deadly force is allowed to stop a thief starting from thirty minutes after sunset until thirty minutes before sunrise. The user of deadly force also has to reasonably believe that the "property cannot be protected or recovered by any other means" or that the "use of force other than deadly force . . . would expose the actor or another to a substantial risk of death or serious bodily injury."

This is an incredibly broad authorization to use deadly force. Imagine that a thief has broken into your garage during the night and grabbed your favorite leaf blower. You manage to catch sight of the thief as he is running away from you and heading toward an accomplice in a getaway car. He's fifty yards from you—too far to close the gap on foot, but just within range to hit him with a 40-caliber piece of hot lead. As he is jumping into the getaway car, you shoot and kill him. This is technically legal in Texas.

The rule of law in the United States is several centuries old, and many strange, archaic laws still exist in our legal codes. Some of them are totally ridiculous. For example, in Tennessee, a law makes it illegal to hold public office if you've ever been in a duel. In one Oregon county, it is illegal to practice fortunetelling or astrology. We normally think of these laws as "fun" and "quirky," merely silly reminders of a past that once was. Seldom, if ever, are they actually enforced. But that's not the case with the Texas deadly force law. Buckle up.

In 2009, Ezekiel Gilbert, a resident of San Antonio, paid an escort he found on Craigslist $150 for what he thought would be a titillating night of paid-for sex. Instead, the escort ended up leaving Gilbert's apartment after twenty minutes, without consummating the act. Angered, Gilbert followed the escort outside and demanded his money back. The escort then fled toward a car driven by the owner of the escort service. As the escort got into the vehicle, Gilbert shot her in the neck through the passenger-side window. The escort was instantly paralyzed and ultimately died from her injuries a few months later at only twenty-three years old.

A Texas jury found that his actions were . . .

Wait for it . . .

Are you ready?

Are you really sure?

Okay, fine.

The jury found that Gilbert's actions were legal. We can return to deadly force law in Texas to see why. Pursuant to Texas law, Gilbert was allowed to use deadly force to prevent a thief from fleeing with his property—during nighttime hours—if he reasonably believed that his property could not be recovered by any other means. Apparently, because the escort was about to flee in a car, the jury found that Gilbert was reasonable to believe that deadly force was the only way to recover his property. Perhaps even more shocking, the jury apparently considered the escort fleeing with Gilbert's $150 to be a theft of his property, even though his underlying transaction (paying for prostitution) was illegal.

Stand Your Ground vs. Duty to Retreat Laws

By this point, we have covered the basic principles of self-defense, the general standard for using deadly force, and some special state laws that expand the use of deadly force to some curious areas. Before wrapping up this topic, let's discuss one more wrinkle in the self-defense analysis.

Most of you have likely heard of "stand your ground" laws. Such laws received immense national attention following the shooting death of Trayvon Martin in Florida in 2012. To best understand stand your ground laws, it's actually most helpful to first discuss the alternative: "duty to retreat" laws.

Some states impose a duty to retreat before you are able to use deadly force in self-defense. Just as it sounds, these states won't allow you to resort to deadly force if you can safely avoid the harm (for example, by running away or calling for help). Only if you were cornered, with no available options of retreat or help, and facing an imminent threat of great bodily injury or death would you be authorized to use deadly force.

Stand your ground laws allow for precisely the opposite. So long as an individual is in a place they are legally entitled to be, any duty to retreat is explicitly eliminated. The initial purpose of these laws was to remove the often-confusing analysis about whether or not a user of deadly force actually had an opportunity to retreat. The rise of these laws is a relatively new phenomenon. Florida was the first to pass such a law in 2005. Today, the popularity of such laws has grown, with more than half of all states having implemented some version of a stand your ground law.

CRASH COURSE

The Trayvon Martin Case Actually Had Nothing to Do with Stand Your Ground Laws

The death of Trayvon Martin in 2012 elicited profound anger throughout the nation. A lot of that anger ended up being directed at Florida's stand your ground law. Indeed, following the death of Martin, a wave of protests and activism targeted the repeal of the law. Even today, a simple Google search of "Trayvon Martin stand your ground law" will return hundreds of articles. However, while many might harbor grievances with the law in general, it actually had no legal relevance in the trial that followed Martin's death.

As many of you will recall, Martin was an unarmed seventeen-year-old African American who was shot and killed by George Zimmerman. At the time of the shooting, Zimmerman was acting as the self-appointed neighborhood watchperson in the gated community where both he and Martin lived. Zimmerman claimed self-defense, but the killing spawned outrage throughout the country. Although Zimmerman faced murder charges, he was ultimately acquitted by a Florida jury.

According to Zimmerman's version of events, Martin had attacked him and ended up on top of him, pinning him to the ground and repeatedly striking him in the face (remember this aspect—it's important). Allegedly fearing for his life, Zimmerman fired one fatal shot to Martin's chest. The validity of this account is hotly contested; Martin, after all, isn't here to share his side of the story. Many also criticize the fact that Zimmerman was out "patrolling" his neighborhood at all, and vehemently claim that he racially profiled Martin. Despite all this, the Florida jury found that Zimmerman reasonably believed he was facing an imminent threat of great bodily harm or death, and that his use of deadly force was therefore justified.

Here's the thing: during the actual trial of Zimmerman, the issue of him legally "standing his ground" was never actually litigated. Zimmerman's defense attorneys never once even argued the issue. This is because, according to Zimmerman's version of events, he had been pinned down by Martin at the time he was attacked. This effectively meant that Zimmerman had no opportunity to retreat, and therefore obviated the need to even apply Florida's stand your ground law. Zimmerman was acquitted under the "general standard" of deadly force, which is the same throughout the entire country.

Some might argue that the mere existence of Florida's stand your ground law, assuming Zimmerman knew of it, still ultimately affected Zimmerman's mental calculus while patrolling his neighborhood and stalking Martin. While this is certainly a valid point, the fact remains that Florida's stand your ground law was never implicated in Zimmerman's trial. Bad media reporting and confusion around the law is primarily to blame for these laws being associated with the case of Trayvon Martin.

Your Home Is Your Castle
The Castle Doctrine

Imagine: You're suddenly awakened in the middle of the night by the sound of your front door being kicked open. You sit up in your bed, sweat instantly forming in the palms of your hands as you hear footsteps and muffled voices in your downstairs living room. Your first thought flashes to your children asleep in the bedroom beside yours. Almost unconsciously, as if rehearsed one thousand times before, you barrel roll out of bed and retrieve your .357 Magnum from your nightstand. *Sweet move, bro*, you think to yourself.

You creep toward the landing of your stairway as the noises from downstairs become more audible. One slow step after another, your gun drawn, you make your way down the stairs. And then you finally see them. Your fears become realized in the form of three masked men, flashlights in hand, burglarizing your home.

But they don't see you yet. Perched in darkness from the stairs above, you have all the advantage. It's the perfect shot. You aim your gun down at the intruders. Your breathing stops as your finger dutifully awaits the order to pull. To shoot, or not to shoot, that is the question.

In terms of legal liability, the answer to that question depends entirely on your state's "castle doctrine."

Nearly every state has adopted what is referred to as a castle doctrine. The name is an homage to the seventeenth-century English philosophy that every man is the king of his "castle." The castle doctrine affords special rights to use deadly force against an intruder in your home. Importantly, each state has its own unique version of the doctrine, with some offering much greater legal protections when confronting home intruders than others. States with a very broad castle doctrine permit the use of deadly force against almost any person who has broken into your home, while other states take a much narrower approach. Each state also defines a "home" slightly differently, with some states including more than just houses and apartments, but also RVs, vehicles, sheds, and boats.

This area of law is truly impossible to generalize, due to the varying intricacies of each state's law. Thus, it's best to simply look at some illustrative examples.

Florida has one of the broadest castle doctrines in the country. In Florida, if someone breaks into your home, the law automatically presumes that you had a reasonable belief of imminent great bodily harm or death (i.e., the general standard is presumptively satisfied). The law operates this way because it presumes that anyone who breaks into someone else's home does so with the intent to commit an act of serious physical violence. Practically speaking, this "presumption of reasonableness" is a very powerful legal tool for any resident using deadly force. A criminal case against such a resident would only be successful if a prosecutor could show with very strong evidence that the resident's imminent fear of great bodily harm or death was actually unreasonable. Any ambiguity or question about the reasonableness of the resident's action must legally fall in their favor.

Nevertheless, the presumption of reasonableness is just that: a presumption. It is not infallible. The presumption can always be rebutted at trial. For example, suppose it's daylight hours and a senile ninety-year-old grandma accidentally breaks into your home and starts asking you for sugar and flour. Obviously, using deadly force against the poor grandma would be so egregious that it would overcome any presumption of reasonableness.

Importantly, the presumption of reasonableness also has a few exceptions. Most notably, the presumption does not apply when using deadly force against a police officer engaged in the performance of official duties. If a police officer intrudes into your home, but properly identifies him or herself, or if you reasonably should have known that the intruder was a police officer, then the presumption of reasonableness for deadly force no longer applies. The presumption also does not apply when using deadly force against any other member of the household, or if you are engaging in criminal activities at the time of using deadly force.

A handful of other states, such as Mississippi, North Carolina, Pennsylvania, and Wisconsin, operate with similar presumptions of reasonableness, albeit with slight variations. Overall, in these states, a resident will be legally justified in shooting most people who break into their home.

In Colorado, things are a bit feisty—the state actually refers to its castle doctrine as the "make my day" law. Under Colorado law, if someone breaks into your home, you are permitted to use deadly force so long as you have a reasonable belief that the intruder "might use any physical force, no matter how slight, against any occupant." As you can imagine, the verbiage "no matter how slight" allows for some pretty wide latitude in using deadly force. If someone breaks into a Colorado home and presents themselves in even the slightest of threatening manners, a resident can use deadly force against them. By contrast, if a ten-year-old girl happens to sneak through a window in order to play with her neighbor's dog, the neighbor (thankfully!) cannot use deadly force because any belief that the child might pose a threat would be unreasonable.

Maine has what we can call a "moderate" castle doctrine. The law makes it "easier" to use deadly force within your home, but it still imposes some significant restrictions before you can do so. Specifically, deadly force can be used when reasonably necessary to prevent an intruder from committing a crime while inside your home. However, before deadly force can be used, you typically have to demand that the intruder leave your property. Deadly force is then only justified if the intruder doesn't immediately comply with your demand. Maine's castle doctrine seeks to strike a balance between giving residents the opportunity to defend themselves and intruders the opportunity to cease their criminal activities before getting killed.

Now, let's look at another state—Massachusetts—with a very limited castle doctrine. To understand Massachusetts' castle doctrine, you must first think back to our discussion of "stand your ground" and "duty to retreat" laws. Massachusetts law generally imposes a duty to retreat before using deadly force in self-defense. However, the state's castle doctrine eliminates this duty while in your own home. That's actually pretty much all the law does—inside your home, you may use deadly force, without needing to first retreat, if you reasonably believe that you are facing an imminent threat of great bodily harm or death (the "general standard"). Many other states, such as Maryland, Minnesota, and New York, have similar castle doctrines that simply remove the duty to retreat while inside the home.

When analyzing the castle doctrine, it's certainly very important to determine, legally speaking, when you are actually *inside* your home. If you are outside of the legally established confines of the home, any protections offered by the castle doctrine go out the window. Different states set different rules for what counts as inside the home.

In the famous New York case of <u>People v. Aiken</u>, Richard Aiken and his neighbor were engaged in a decade-long squabble. In fact, following one particularly heated verbal exchange, the neighbor literally stabbed Aiken in the back, hospitalizing him for two days. In the ensuing years, the neighbor repeatedly threatened to shoot, stab, or otherwise harm Aiken. Finally, one day, the fighting between Aiken and his neighbor reached its zenith. Aiken and his neighbor were arguing in Aiken's doorway when the neighbor walked up to Aiken, pressed his face against him, and told him that he was going to kill him. Allegedly fearing for his life, Aiken hit his neighbor in the head with a large metal pipe, killing him. The court ruled that the castle doctrine did not apply because Aiken was not inside his home. Specifically, the court rejected Aiken's argument that his doorway was part of his home. He was eventually convicted of manslaughter and sentenced to sixteen years in prison. In contrast to New York, Pennsylvania law considers one's doorway, deck, or patio as part of the home for castle doctrine purposes. Florida even extends castle doctrine protections to fenced backyards.

Let's now wrap up this quick topic by returning to our hypothetical home intruder situation.

There you are again—perched atop your stairs, gun in hand, watching three masked men burglarize your home after having kicked in your front door. Can you legally shoot them? If you happen to live in a state with a castle doctrine that includes a presumption of reasonableness, such as in Florida, odds are very good that your shooting would be justified. Under Colorado's expansive law requiring only a reasonable belief that the intruders might use (even the slightest) physical force, you are also probably justified to shoot. Under Maine's more moderate castle doctrine, you must first give the intruders an opportunity to leave before shooting them. In states with more restricted castle doctrines, such as Massachusetts, you must reasonably believe that you are facing an imminent threat of great bodily harm or death before you can shoot—but you at least do not have to retreat. In Massachusetts, the use of deadly force would be highly questionable. After all, at this point you haven't seen that the intruders possess any weapons, and they have not made any threats toward you. For all you know, they might scurry away at the simple sight of your presence. It would be up to a jury to decide if your belief of imminent great bodily harm or death was reasonable.

Boobytraps Are Totally Illegal
Mechanical Defensive Devices

You know darn well that you've thought about it before: *are boobytraps legal?* Unfortunately, *Home Alone* lied to you—they're not!

Let's orient our boobytrap discussion around the seminal case Katko v. Briney. Edward and Bertha Briney owned a farmhouse in rural Iowa. Although they did not live at the farmhouse (their actual home was a few miles away), Mr. Briney watched after the property, and the family stored many of their heirlooms inside. For nearly a decade, the Brineys dealt with a scourge of repeated break-ins and drug-using trespassers. They tried installing new locks, putting up fences, and erecting signs declaring "no trespassing," all to no avail. Finally reaching his wit's end, Mr. Briney set up a spring gun boobytrap in one of the bedrooms. The boobytrap consisted of a shotgun pointed at the bedroom door that was rigged to fire if the door was opened. "That'll teach 'em," Mr. Briney no doubt smirked to himself.

But it was Mr. Briney who would ultimately learn a lesson.

One summer night in 1967, while the farmhouse was unoccupied, Marvin Katko made his move. Katko illegally entered the farmhouse and began stealing some of the items inside. Upon entering the bedroom, he was shot in the leg by the shotgun boobytrap. Katko's injuries were serious and he required extensive hospitalization. Shortly after his release from the hospital, Katko sued the Brineys for the injuries he sustained.

The legality of Mr. Briney's boobytrap wound up being litigated in the Iowa Supreme Court. There, the court ruled that using deadly force on intruders in an unoccupied property was never reasonable (remember, deadly force need not necessitate that someone actually die). As explained by the Court, had Mr. Briney been physically present when Katko broke into his farmhouse, it's possible that the use of deadly force would have been justified, because Mr. Briney could have perceived an imminent threat of great bodily harm or death. However, without a human being present or in actual danger, the use of deadly force can't ever be reasonable. Katko won his lawsuit and the Brineys were forced to pay him $30,000 (about $200,000 in today's dollars).

Years after the case was decided, Mr. Briney was asked during an interview if he would change anything about the situation. Mr. Briney replied, "I'd have aimed that gun a few feet higher." In a fit of blissful irony, Katko's own home was burglarized several years later.

Since <u>Katko v. Briney</u>, it has become widely recognized in the United States that setting boobytraps to protect property—whether deadly or not—is illegal. Indeed, several people have even been convicted of murder for setting such traps. In one recent case from Illinois in 2019, William Wasmund was found guilty of murder when the shotgun boobytrap he had set up to protect a shed on his property killed an intruder. Wasmund was ultimately sentenced to thirty years in prison.

But ... Why?

So why aren't boobytraps permitted? *It's my land, stay out! I thought this was America!*

Courts have offered a multitude of justifications for the prohibition on boobytraps, the most common being that certain people have a legal right (and need) to enter your home without permission, such as firefighters, police, and paramedics. In the recent Illinois case mentioned above, the local police department advocated strongly for charging Wasmund with murder. They feared that if boobytraps were allowed any leniency, their officers might encounter one while responding to an emergency.

But emergency personnel are not the only people who might step foot onto someone's property without permission. Some unlucky passerby might also wander into someone's shed to find shelter in a thunderstorm, or a little boy might stumble onto someone's property to find his lost baseball. Because the law takes the view that boobytraps are illegal, we don't have to live in a society with potential danger lurking on our neighbor's lawn.

From a legal analysis, boobytraps are also problematic because they are . . . well, not human. If you think back to our discussion on the legal requirements for the use of self-defense, you will remember that nearly all self-defense laws, even non-deadly self-defense, include a calculation of reasonableness. Because boobytraps are merely machines incapable of assessing situations or making judgments, they are not sufficiently able to perceive what is reasonable and what is not.

Finally, the prohibition on boobytraps also exists to protect the would-be setter of the trap. Boobytraps are inherently dangerous devices that could easily end up injuring the person setting them. A few years ago in North Carolina, a man who had set up boobytraps around his home accidentally shot himself when he triggered one of them. According to police reports, the man had opened his backdoor to feed the squirrels he saw in his yard. And that's when the boobytrap went off. "The squirrels did me in," the man reportedly told 9-1-1 operators.

SECTION 4: YOUR RIGHTS

Abortions Are Actually All About . . . Privacy?
The Right of Privacy

In 1969, Norma McCorvey—using the pseudonym Jane Roe—was pregnant in the state of Texas and wanted an abortion. However, under Texas law at the time, abortions were illegal unless they were necessary to save the mother's life. McCorvey filed a lawsuit against the local prosecutor (Henry Wade), alleging that the Texas law was unconstitutional. (McCorvey eventually gave birth and put her child up for adoption while her case went forward.) A few years later, the infamous case of Roe v. Wade found itself in front of the Supreme Court. The Court ultimately ruled that the Constitution protects a woman's choice to have to an abortion and that states cannot impede this choice with unduly restrictive laws.

Many of you have probably already heard a great deal about Roe v. Wade. Indeed, with the recent appointment of three conservative Supreme Court Justices (Neil Gorsuch, Brett Kavanaugh, and the religiously outspoken Amy Coney Barrett), Roe has been pushed firmly into the national spotlight, as those in the "pro-choice" camp worry that the seminal case could be overturned.

But what many of you probably don't know is why Roe was decided the way that it was (i.e., which constitutional right actually protects abortions?). Surprising to most, the answer is actually the "right to privacy." In essence, the Court in Roe reasoned that the Constitution included a right to privacy, and this privacy right prevented the government from intruding into a woman's choice to have an abortion. If you've ever read the Constitution, however, you may notice one elephant-sized problem here:

The Constitution says absolutely nothing about privacy.

Let's go ahead and try to figure this one out.

The idea that the Constitution includes a right to privacy first gained traction eight years before Roe, in the case Griswold v. Connecticut. Here, the Supreme Court struck down a state law banning the use of contraceptives among married couples. The Court reasoned that such a law was improper because the Constitution included a right to privacy, which protected against government intrusion into intimate marital issues. Acknowledging that the Constitution never actually says anything about privacy, the Court nevertheless found that the right to privacy existed in the "penumbras" of the Constitution. The word penumbra is derived from Latin and can be loosely defined as "partial shadow." (It's pronounced puh·nuhm·bruh, in case you want to impress your friends, bruh.)

What the Court actually meant here is that several of the explicitly enumerated rights found in the Constitution form, by implication, other rights that are not actually mentioned. Specifically, the Ninth Amendment states that the "enumeration in the Constitution of certain rights shall not be construed to deny or disparage other rights retained by the people." Courts have taken the Ninth Amendment as a directive to read the Constitution broadly to include additional rights not explicitly articulated in the actual text. These implied (aka "penumbral") rights exist in the "shadows" of the enumerated rights.

As argued by the Court, various enumerated constitutional rights create an implied "zone of privacy." For example, the First Amendment affords privacy in the religious beliefs and speech of citizens. The Third Amendment grants a certain privacy in the home by prohibiting the quartering of soldiers in private residences. The Fourth Amendment explicitly grants citizens the right "to be secure in their persons, houses, papers, and effects" and forbids "unreasonable searches and seizures," just as the Fourteenth Amendment decrees that the government shall not deprive any person of their liberty.

In reading these various constitutional provisions together, the court inferred that a right to privacy was implied. This idea went on to affect several important cases in the proceeding years. In 1969, the Supreme Court held in <u>Stanley v. Georgia</u> that the right to privacy protected a person's right to possess and view adult pornography in their home. In the 2003 case of <u>Lawrence v. Texas</u>, the Supreme Court again relied on the right of privacy when finding that gay men had a legal right to engage in sexual intercourse. (As a quick aside, the date of this case is not a typo—Texas actually criminalized homosexual sex into the twenty-first century.)

Some legal commentators fully support the "penumbral reasoning" employed by the Court in <u>Griswold v. Connecticut</u> and later in <u>Roe v. Wade</u>. These individuals often point to the fact that the right to privacy is not the only right that has been established by implication.

You may have heard that the First Amendment grants the "freedom to associate," but such a freedom is not actually stated in the text. Rather, courts have found that the First Amendment's enumerated guarantees of free speech and the right to petition the government imply that citizens have a right to form political associations. After all, the right to free speech and to petition the government would mean little without the right to freely associate.

At the same time, just as many commentators feel quite the opposite, believing that the right to privacy is an absurd judicial fiction created by the courts in order to justify their personal and socially-based opinions. Others support the general right to privacy, but find its application to the circumstances of abortion inappropriate.

The Landscape of Abortion Laws Today

The rest of our discussion will offer a high-level overview of the general laws on abortion as they exist in the United States today. As the first step, you need to know a little bit more about what the Court in Roe v. Wade specifically held. The opinion is actually extremely dense, complicated, and around thirty pages long, so I'll just give you the highlights.

In affording constitutional protections for abortions, the Court in Roe held that, prior to the point of fetal viability (i.e., the ability of the fetus to live outside the womb), states could not outlaw abortions. But once viability was reached, states had wide latitude in restricting abortions, including banning them outright (so long as exceptions existed for situations when the life or health of the mother was in jeopardy). The Court adopted a trimester framework for explaining what kinds of laws states could pass prior to the point of viability. During the first trimester, states could not restrict abortions at all; the choice to have an abortion was left strictly between the mother and her physician. During the second trimester, states still could not outlaw abortions, but they could impose reasonable regulations in the interest of protecting the health of the mother—for example, passing a law that required abortions to be provided by a licensed physician. During the third trimester, when the fetus was generally considered viable, states could fully outlaw abortions.

Things changed a bit in 1992 when the Supreme Court decided the case of Planned Parenthood v. Casey. Here, the Court reaffirmed the viability standard in Roe v. Wade, holding that states could not outlaw abortions prior to fetal viability. However, the Court changed the framework around what kind of restrictions states could impose prior to viability. The Court did away with using trimesters as reference points, and instead applied one general standard throughout the entire pre-viability portion of pregnancy: states could pass laws regulating abortions so long as they did not place an "undue burden" on the pregnant woman. An undue burden was defined as having the "purpose or effect" of creating "substantial obstacles in the path of a woman seeking an abortion."

Interestingly, while Roe v. Wade is certainly very important as the landmark case that first offered constitutional protections for abortions, Planned Parenthood v. Casey is arguably even more significant, given that it is the current law in place today. However, Casey is seldom given public attention.

For the pro-choice camp, the decision in Casey was both a win and a loss. On the one hand, the Supreme Court had become more conservative than it was during Roe v. Wade, which left open the chance that the Court would overturn Roe entirely. Many rejoiced in the simple fact that the Court upheld the constitutional privacy right that protected abortions. On the other hand, the new "undue burden" standard adopted by the Court was significantly broader and more ambiguous, leaving states with much greater wiggle room to regulate abortions. Now, even the first trimester of pregnancy was fair game.

A few of the standards set in Roe and Casey may seem a bit confusing and unclear. *Viability? Undue burden?* If you're wondering what all these terms mean, you're not alone.

Let's look at this viability standard first. Truth is, a lot of people (conservatives and liberals alike) hate it. In Casey, the late Justice Antonin Scalia authored one of his most famous blistering dissents, proclaiming that the Court's ruling was "inherently manipulable" and "hopelessly unworkable." Neither Roe nor Casey set out any defined timetables to determine when viability actually exists.

So . . . how do we know when a fetus is viable?

Taking a look at a few state statutes, viability has been defined as occurring when, "in the good faith medical judgment of a physician, on the particular facts of the case before that physician, there is a reasonable likelihood of the fetus' sustained survival outside the uterus without the application of extraordinary medical measures."

There you go! Crystal clear! *Right?! No?* Okay, fair.

Many legal commentators argue that fetal viability presents an impracticable legal standard because the determination of viability is so nebulous and fact-specific. Indeed, the medical community recognizes that viability can be influenced by a multitude of factors, such as race, gender, whether the mother smokes, the medical technology available at the time, and even the altitude of where the mother lives. Worse so, the entire concept of viability can be subjective; different physicians can disagree as to when a specific fetus has progressed to the state of viability.

Despite its potential flaws, courts have routinely emphasized that fetal viability is the crucial marker when the scales tip and the government's interest in promoting a viable human life outweighs a woman's constitutional right to an abortion. While many can understand the logic behind setting this standard, the practical application of actually enforcing the law has drawn extensive scrutiny.

Got it. Now, what kind of abortion restrictions place an "undue burden" on a woman?

The concept of "undue burden" has likewise been chastised as extremely ambiguous. The dissenting Supreme Court Justices in <u>Casey</u> argued that the undue burden standard would force judges to make entirely subjective and unguided determinations, likely leading to conflict around an already emotionally charged issue. At its core, the undue burden standard is a balancing test. The standard requires judges to weigh the burdens a law imposes on abortion access against the benefits that those laws confer. If burdens outweigh benefits, the law is unconstitutional. While this sort of balancing test might seem inherently subjective, it is the role of the impartial judge to undertake this calculus. Someone has to do it! The undue burden standard is not unique to abortion and has been used to analyze many different questions of constitutional law. For example, in <u>Morgan v. Virginia</u>, the Supreme Court applied an undue burden test to find that Virginia's law enforcing school segregation on interstate buses was unconstitutional.

According to the pro-choice camp, conservative state governments have capitalized on this ambiguity of the undue burden standard by sneaking through extremely restrictive laws. Many very restrictive laws have been upheld under the theory that they provide a significant benefit by protecting the health of the mother. Over the last few decades, the Supreme Court has invalidated abortion restrictions on only a handful of occasions.

The actual facts of <u>Planned Parenthood v. Casey</u> offer a good example. In 1982, Pennsylvania passed the Abortion Control Act, which included several restrictions on abortions. Specifically, the law imposed a twenty-four-hour waiting period, the mandatory dissemination of abortion-related information to the mother, parental consent for minors, and a requirement that married women notify their husbands before having an abortion. Planned Parenthood sued to challenge the law. According to the Supreme Court, most aspects of this law did not present an undue burden. The twenty-four-hour waiting period, mandatory dissemination of information, and parental consent requirement conferred the important benefit of well-considered abortions without unduly restricting access to them. By contrast, the husband notification requirement was found to be an undue burden. The requirement presented an extreme obstacle to abortions because husbands could prevent them through physical force, psychological pressure, or economic coercion. At the same time, the Court reasoned that the requirement served no legitimate benefit because a husband has no lawful right to require his wife to advise him before she exercises her personal choices.

Another notable example of the Supreme Court invalidating an abortion restriction occurred in the 2016 case of <u>Whole Woman's Health v. Hellerstedt</u>. Here, the Court invalidated provisions of a Texas law that required (1) doctors who perform abortions to have difficult-to-obtain "admitting privileges" at a local hospital, and (2) clinics to have nearly hospital-grade facilities and equipment. Those in the pro-choice camp vehemently opposed the law, given that its enforcement would have caused the majority of abortion clinics in the state to close. Conversely, the state of Texas argued that the law provided the important benefit of reducing the amount of dangerous abortions performed under substandard medical conditions.

A gruesome case from Pennsylvania involving physician and abortion provider, Dr. Kermit Gosnell, allegedly formed the backbone of the law. Years earlier, Dr. Gosnell had been convicted of murdering several born-alive infants. He was also convicted of manslaughter for the death of one woman that occurred during an abortion procedure. His trial revealed utterly shocking and abhorrent details about the hundreds of illegal late-term abortions he performed, including overdosing his patients with dangerous drugs while inducing labor and spreading venereal diseases with non-sanitized instruments.

Although acknowledging the horrific case of Dr. Gosnell, the Court found no evidence that the Texas law would prevent such an occurrence from happening again. As stated by the Court: "Determined wrongdoers, already ignoring existing statutes and safety measures, are unlikely to be convinced to adopt safe practices by a new overlay of regulations." Rather, the Court found that the Texas law offered very minimal, if any, health benefits to women, and its enforcement would create an immense burden on access to abortions by closing down the majority of clinics within the state. The scales tipped in favor of invalidating the law.

The Rise of the Incrementalistic Hodgepodge

Over the past few decades, states have slowly passed laws regulating how, when, and under what circumstances a woman may obtain an abortion. By enacting one law at a time, with each individual law passing muster under the "undue burden" standard, more conservative states have ended up with an overall legal landscape that many would argue makes abortions very difficult to attain. Indeed, some "pro-life" supporters have specifically articulated this "incremental approach" as a tactic to eventually overturn the constitutional protections for abortion, the idea being to chip away at abortion rights until the current constitutional protections become so incoherent and full of holes that courts just get rid of them altogether.

Let's look at some common regulations of today:

Physician Requirements: Forty states require that an abortion be performed by a licensed physician (rather than a nurse or physician assistant, for example).

State-Mandated Counseling and Information: Eighteen states mandate that women be given counseling before an abortion, including information on at least one of the following: the purported link between abortion and breast cancer (five states), the ability of a fetus to feel pain (thirteen states), or long-term mental health consequences for the woman (eight states).

State-Mandated Ultrasounds: Three states—Louisiana, Texas, and Wisconsin—mandate that an abortion provider perform an ultrasound on every woman seeking an abortion, and also requires the provider to specifically show and describe the image to the woman.

Waiting Periods: Twenty-seven states require a woman to wait a specified period of time, often twenty-four hours, between her first contact with an abortion provider and when the abortion is performed.

Parental Involvement: Thirty-seven states require some type of parental involvement in a minor's decision to have an abortion.

Gestational Limits: This last one is especially important. Forty-three states outlaw abortions after a specified point in pregnancy. Remember, Roe and Casey ruled that post-viability, states can fully outlaw abortions. But with viability left undefined by the Courts, several states have taken it upon themselves to set their own timeframes for viability. Nineteen states currently outlaw abortions at twenty weeks, even though the medical community generally views viability as occurring at around twenty-four weeks. The constitutionality of these "twenty-week bans" is hotly contested. In fact, North Carolina's twenty-week ban was recently found to be unconstitutional by a federal judge.

On the other hand, several states have never actually passed any law setting a time restriction on abortions. Roe and Casey ruled that states can outlaw abortions post-viability, but didn't actually require them to do so. This is a particularly shocking fact for many people: several states technically allow for the possibility that an abortion could be performed weeks, days, or even hours prior to birth. Pro-choice supporters would argue that such laws don't reflect the real-life practice of abortions, citing studies that show less than one percent of abortions take place after twenty-four weeks. They might also point to the importance of such laws in the case that a mother discovers late during her pregnancy that the fetus has serious genetic abnormalities. Further, few (if any) physicians would actually be willing to perform an abortion so late in the pregnancy. Despite these arguments, some pro-life supporters still find themselves extremely discomforted by the reality that some states technically allow abortions up until the moment of birth.

Overall, as conservative states have been enacting abortion time limits and other types of restrictions, liberal states have been doing the exact opposite and working to increase opportunities and legal protections. This sort of wild variance among state laws has resulted in a confusing hodgepodge across the country, so let's end our overview on abortion laws by taking a look at some of the current laws in three states from across the political spectrum: Oregon (generally liberal), Virginia (generally moderate), and Mississippi (generally conservative).

	Oregon	Virginia	Mississippi
Abortion must be performed by licensed physician	No	Yes	Yes
Timeframe after which abortions are outlawed	None	Start of third trimester	20 weeks
Mandated counseling and information for mother	None	Yes	Yes
Waiting period	None	24 hours	24 hours
Ultrasound required	No	No	Yes
Parental notice and consent for minors	Neither	Notice and consent	Notice and consent

The Legal Landscape of the Future

What would happen if Roe v. Wade were overturned?

This question is asked today more than ever, perhaps justifiably so. It is only a matter of time until the Supreme Court hears a new abortion case and has an opportunity to overrule the constitutional protections first outlined in Roe. During the past few years, a handful of "rogue" states have passed extremely hostile abortion laws, such as Georgia's "heartbeat" law, which bans abortions at around six weeks. None of these laws have actually gone into effect because they are being challenged in court. Oddly enough, some suggest that this is precisely the plan for such laws. Given that they are objectively illegal, they will be litigated in court and provide an opportunity for appeal to the Supreme Court. Upon review, the Supreme Court might then re-examine Roe and overrule it entirely.

It is important to note, however, that the Supreme Court is never required to hear a particular case. Even when a litigant has gone through all the proper channels to finally appeal a decision to the Supreme Court, the Court can always decline to hear the case. The Court receives around seven thousand requests to hear cases each year, but only decides around one hundred of them. Given the Supreme Court's discretion in deciding which cases it hears, it is impossible to predict when the next review of Roe might take place.

If Roe were to be overruled one day, the power to legalize (or outlaw) abortion would return to individual states. It's important to understand that overruling Roe would *not* make abortions automatically illegal throughout the country. This is a misconception. Rather, states would have all the power to decide whether abortions are legal or illegal and how they should be regulated. As discussed previously, states across the country already diverge significantly in their laws regulating abortion. Absent Roe, such divergence would simply be amplified. The opportunities for abortions in California compared to Louisiana would be worlds apart.

In the absence of Roe, Congress might eventually step in and pass a law to legalize or outlaw abortions nationwide. Some suggest that congressional action is actually the best option, given that policy decisions are supposed to be vested with the legislature, and not with the courts. Even some in the pro-choice camp support the idea of abortion being taken out of the courtroom. This is because more favorable laws could be crafted by a democratically elected Congress compared to the decisions made by the Supreme Court, which is comprised of nine presidentially appointed members. Additionally, given that the "right to privacy" basis underpinning Roe has come under such severe criticism, a new law passed by Congress could have better support to stand against its opponents.

You Can Legally Steal Someone's Land if You Keep It Long Enough
Adverse Possession

The right to own land is sacred in Western cultures and their laws. For centuries, land ownership has been seen as the pinnacle of wealth and power. At the time the Declaration of Independence was signed, only those who owned land had the right to vote. Land ownership and general property rights have also been important catalysts in developing societies for fostering individual liberty and economic stability. As noted by John Adams in 1790, "Property must be secured or liberty cannot exist."

Given the cherished status of land ownership, it may surprise you that your land can actually be stolen from you—legally.

Adverse Possession

Under the doctrine of adverse possession, a trespasser can come onto your land, occupy it, and eventually gain legal ownership of it. Every state has its own specific requirements for gaining ownership via adverse possession, but generally speaking, courts will look at four factors. To qualify as adverse possession, the trespasser's occupation of the land must be:

(1) Hostile: "Hostile" doesn't necessarily mean that you enter the property while beating your fists against your chest and proclaiming your ultimate dominance via megaphone. Indeed, most states just define "hostile" as simply occupying the land. (Kind of a weird definition of hostile, but that is the status of the law.) Some states do ask for a bit more actual hostility and at least require that the trespasser knows the land they are occupying belongs to someone else.

(2) Actual: This prong requires that the trespasser "actually" possesses the land. As in, the trespasser is actually present on the land and treats the land as if he or she owns it. This is commonly proven by documenting attempts to maintain or improve the land. For example, are you regularly cutting the grass?

(3) Open and notorious: "Open and notorious" means that it must be obvious to anyone, including the "real" property owner, that a trespasser is on the land. The most common example is a trespasser erecting a new fence around the occupied property. Courts will also sometimes look to the beliefs of people in the community. Is your use of the land so open and notorious that everyone else in town presumes you own it?

(4) Exclusive and continuous: Finally, the trespasser must possess the land "exclusively," meaning that they are not sharing the land with other parties. The possession must also be "continuous." Put simply, this just means that the trespasser uses the land as one normally would for a continuous, non-broken length of time. Different states require different time periods of exclusive and continuous use in order to succeed on claims of adverse possession. For example, Oregon requires ten years, whereas New Jersey requires thirty years.

Let's now dive into at least one real-world example. Nome 2000 v. Fagerstrom is a famous case of adverse possession from the state of Alaska. Nome 2000 was a mining company that owned 7.5 acres of land in the Alaskan forest. The Fagerstroms were a family that lived near Nome 2000's land and, for over thirty years, routinely used several acres on the northern portion of the plot for recreational purposes. The Fagerstroms built an outhouse and a cabin on the northern acres, parked their trailer there, maintained the area, and even excluded others from using the land. Nome 2000 eventually came to realize that the Fagerstroms had been using their land and sued the family in an attempt to eject them from it. The Fagerstroms counterclaimed that they had acquired ownership of the land via adverse possession. *Classic Fagerstroms*. Ultimately, the Court agreed with the Fagerstroms because:

(1) The Fagerstroms' use of the land was hostile. In Alaska, hostility is defined as simply using the land without permission, and the Fagerstroms had no permission to use the land.

(2) The Fagerstroms actually used the land as if they owned it—they erected new structures, maintained the land, and kept others out.

(3) The Fagerstroms' use of the land was open and notorious. The construction of the cabin and outhouse, as well as the parked trailer, gave Nome 2000 "constructive notice" that someone else was clearly living on the land. Constructive notice is a legal term that means something has been made so obvious that any reasonable person would know about it. If constructive notice is satisfied, then it doesn't matter if the individual actually knew about it or not. This concept prevents individuals from deliberately sticking their heads in the sand in order to avoid various notice requirements.

(4) The Fagerstroms' use of the land was sufficiently exclusive and continuous. The use of the land was not shared with other parties, and the Fagerstroms used the land for over thirty years. In Alaska, adverse possession requires exclusive and continuous use of the land for only ten years.

And there you have it. Although Nome 2000 had legally purchased the land and presumably wished to use it one day for its mining business, the Fagerstroms usurped ownership over the northern acres. The maxim "use it or lose it" is one that should be heeded by property owners.

But . . . Why?

Adverse possession lawsuits rarely end up being litigated in court. Although it's not as flashy and exciting, the most common adverse possession cases involve very small boundary issues, usually amongst neighbors. For example, let's say your home driveway just slightly overruns onto your neighbor's property, but no one actually realizes it for twenty years until your neighbors put their house up for sale and take a look at the property's plat map. You've likely acquired this area of the driveway via adverse possession. Still, no one wants to drag their neighbors into court, so you'll probably choose to just settle the issue amongst yourselves.

A handful of states are also moving away from the doctrine and making it much harder for would-be adverse possessors to actually take ownership of someone else's land. California has taken the very significant step of requiring an adverse possessor to show that he or she paid state taxes on the subject property for five years before acquiring ownership of it. Thus, almost all adverse possession cases fail in California.

Still, one might ask why the doctrine even exists at all. *I mean . . . bro, I paid for this land; what makes you think you can have it? I have an old pair of jeans I haven't worn in a while, do you want those too?!*

Adverse possession is supported by the philosophy that land is an incredibly valuable asset, and it's always better that someone, rather than no one, is at least using it. Ironically, it is because property rights are so valuable that they can be taken away from you. Assuming that an adverse possessor has actually been using the land exclusively and for a significant length of time, it is likely that they have built a genuine reliance and relationship with the land. Some view it as unfair to oust them from the land when the "real" landowners have completely neglected it. Remember, the requirements for adverse possession are a significant hurdle. It might not be appropriate to view the real landowner as "at fault," but they must be, at a minimum, seriously neglectful of their land in order for an adverse possessor to rightfully take ownership. In the case of <u>Nome 2000 v. Fagerstrom</u>, Nome 2000 apparently didn't bother to check on their land for thirty years.

And finally, adverse possession finds support in the concept of statutes of limitations. In the United States, the vast majority of laws have a statute of limitations for bringing criminal charges or a civil lawsuit. This means that the law sets a maximum amount of time after an event takes place for legal actions to be brought. As an example, in North Dakota there is a six-year statute of limitations for personal injury cases. If someone hurts you in North Dakota and you want to sue them for it, you have six years to do it or you're out of luck. By the same token, North Dakota has a three-year statute of limitations for burglary. The government has to charge you with the crime of burglary within three years of you committing the act, or you'll be off scot-free. (Only particularly heinous crimes—such as murder, rape, and terrorism—don't have a statute of limitations.)

The idea behind statutes of limitations is simple: legal grievances should be dealt with in a timely manner. If legal actions are not brought within a reasonable timeframe, pertinent facts and evidence surrounding the issue can become stale and unclear. A robust psychological literature has demonstrated that testifying witnesses are, at a baseline, pretty bad at memory recollection. Asking someone to remember a seemingly inconsequential detail fifteen years after the fact is like trying to ask a toddler to do calculus. Furthermore, old cases could also be used as a means of harassment if there were no time limits in place. *Remember that time I twisted my ankle slipping on your icy stairs ten years go? I'm suing you for it now and it has _absolutely nothing_ to do with the fact that you just posted a really ugly photo of me on Instagram.*

Adverse possession operates as a kind of statute of limitations for the real landowners. If someone is "stealing" your land, the law mandates that you bring a legal action within a reasonable timeframe, or else you might lose your land entirely.

CRASH COURSE

Eminent Domain

We can't discuss land being ripped from right out under your feet without at least mentioning eminent domain. Similar to adverse possession, eminent domain can cause a property owner to lose their land. However, under eminent domain, it is the government doing the taking.

Eminent domain refers to the power of the government to take private property and convert it into public use, most commonly for things like highways, railways, or utility lines. However, the government cannot just go around taking land *willy-nilly*—the Fifth Amendment wouldn't allow it. Indeed, the Fifth Amendment explicitly states, "nor shall private property be taken for public use, without just compensation." This part of the Fifth Amendment is regularly referred to as the "Takings Clause."

The Takings Clause is comprised of two separate mandates. First, the government can only take private property if it is to be used for public purposes. Second, the government must pay the landowner "just compensation" for their land. At a high-level, the requirement for just compensation is actually pretty straightforward. Courts have interpreted just compensation to mean the price that an average buyer would pay an average seller in a voluntary transaction (i.e., the "fair market value"). The public use requirement, on the other hand, has been a source of significant controversy. Let's look at two notable examples.

In Berman v. Parker, the District of Columbia wished to take a large area of private property—about an entire neighborhood—in order to clear the many "blighted" (i.e., dilapidated or unsightly) properties from the city. Once the government took the property via eminent domain, it was to be transferred to a private redevelopment company that would demolish the structures and build condominiums, private office buildings, and a shopping center in their place. The owners of a department store, which was not itself deemed blighted but nonetheless caught within the overall redevelopment plan, sued to challenge the eminent domain action. Although the properties were to be transferred to a private redeveloper who stood to receive a financial windfall, the Court still found that the taking of the neighborhood constituted a public use because making the nation's capital "beautiful" served a sufficient public purpose.

Fifty years after the Berman decision, the Supreme Court went on to interpret the public use requirement even more broadly in Kelo v. City of New London. Here, the city government again endeavored to take a large swatch of property in order to pursue a redevelopment plan. However, these properties were *not* blighted. There was nothing particularly wrong with them; rather, the government simply argued that allowing private developers to repurpose the land would create more jobs and increase tax revenues for the city. Shocking most legal observers, the Court found that such anticipated economic benefits satisfied the public use requirement. As you might imagine, the outcome of the case caused significant backlash and controversy. In her dissent, Justice O'Connor voiced serious concerns regarding the profound effects that such a ruling would have for all owners of private property, stating poignantly, "Nothing is to prevent the State from replacing any Motel 6 with a Ritz-Carlton, any home with a shopping mall, or any farm with a factory." In an embarrassing display of wasted time and energy, the private developer in the case was ultimately unable to obtain financing for the project and, to this day, much of the land remains a barren field. Opponents of the Court's decision find this to be poetic justice.

Before we wrap up this CRASH COURSE, let's talk about a gigantic coal mine fire that has been burning beneath a city for over sixty years. Oh, and eminent domain.

The city of Centralia, Pennsylvania epitomizes the word catastrophe. Once filled with shops, homes, and a prominent mining business, today the city is an abandoned and graffiti-laden ghost town. Most structures have been demolished, and the few still standing have been reclaimed by natural forest growth. In 1962, a fire broke out somewhere in the labyrinth-like coal mines that existed beneath nearly the entire town. The coal mines beneath Centralia were so numerous and prolific that it made isolating and fighting the fire a logistical and financial nightmare. One geologist analyzed the situation and stated that extinguishing the fire was an "impossible dream." While coal mine fires actually occur quite regularly, Centralia's was one of the worst in American history.

As years passed, residents started falling ill from the poisonous gasses seeping from underground. The ground beneath the city became hotter and hotter, reaching over 900 degrees in some places. Reportedly, numerous graves in the town's cemetery dropped into the literal fiery abyss raging below. Houses began to tilt and crumble as the earth shifted and dangerous sinkholes started to emerge, which nearly led to the death of one child.

Suffice it to say, living in Centralia was no longer safe.

So, in 1992, the State of Pennsylvania took ownership over the city via eminent domain, with all property owners receiving just compensation in order to help them move elsewhere. Although most residents willingly took their money and left, a handful apparently wanted to keep living amidst the setting of a horror film. Eight lifelong Centralia residents sued the state in a last-ditch effort to retain the right to live in their homes. Although the state had the power to evict the remaining residents under eminent domain, it decided to allow the eight individuals to continue living in their homes until their deaths (all were quite old).

While Centralia's story might be unique, the promotion of public safety is a common justification when using eminent domain. Interestingly, however, there is no actual legal requirement for the government to keep citizens safe. The Constitution and other foundational laws tend to focus more on preventing the government from hindering one's ability to live freely and safely, with none actually including any mandate for the government to protect its citizens (as we saw during our discussion about the police having no duty to protect). And yet, many of the laws that we might find most annoying (speed limits) or intrusive (TSA screenings at airports) are justified by public safety. The COVID-19 pandemic and resulting lockdowns offer stark examples of broad-sweeping laws enacted in the interest of public safety.

One Vote in Wyoming Is Worth Four in California

The Electoral College

Ah, the Electoral College. What controversy dost thou elicit!
For some, the Electoral College stands as a true mark of ingenuity and a testament to the foresight of our Founding Fathers. For others, the Electoral College represents a system that is unfair, racially discriminatory, and disenfranchising. Over the last few decades, millions of dollars have been poured into initiatives to abolish the system. During her campaign for the Democratic presidential nomination in the 2020 elections, Senator Elizabeth Warren ran on a platform that explicitly called for the abolishment of the Electoral College.

The Electoral College provides the system for the election of the president of the United States. In today's incendiary and divisive political climate, understanding this system is more important than ever.

What is the Electoral College?

So, what is this special Electoral College system?

First, let's talk about what it's not. It is *not* a popular vote system. Most republics and democracies throughout the globe elect their leaders via a national popular vote. Such a system is extremely simple: each eligible citizen gets one vote, all votes from the eligible citizenry are counted, and the candidate with the most total votes wins the election. But in America, that's not how we do things.

Under the Electoral College system, each state—plus the District of Columbia—is allotted a certain number of electoral delegates, who will each cast one electoral vote. The number of delegates each state receives is based on the number of members the state has in Congress.

In total, there are 535 members of Congress: 100 senators (two for every state), and 435 representatives in the House. Federal law requires each state to have two senators and the maximum number of House representatives to be capped at 435. While the overall number of congressional members will not change, the number of representatives apportioned to each state fluctuates quite frequently. Specifically, the number of representatives each state has in the House is based on the population recorded in the national census every ten years. Fun fact: this is why the collection of data during the census is often a cause for controversy! You can see what kind of immense power census data might wield. Simply speaking, more populated states will be apportioned more members in the House. For example, Illinois has eighteen House representatives, whereas Alaska has only one.

To make sure we've really nailed this down, let's look at Iowa's representation in the Electoral College. Iowa has six seats in Congress. Specifically, it has four members in the House of Representatives and two senators. This means that Iowa is allotted six electoral delegates, who will cast six electoral votes for the president. Because each state has *at least* one member in the House of Representatives and two senators, the smallest number of electoral delegates a state can possibly possess is three. With every new national census, each state's number of electoral votes is subject to change due to population growth or decline. For example, since 1976, Texas has gained twelve electoral delegates, while New York has lost twelve.

Importantly, although the Electoral College as a whole does not utilize the popular vote, states use a popular vote to determine who their electoral delegates ultimately vote for. In simpler terms, when a candidate gets the majority of a state's popular vote, *all* electoral votes in that state go to that candidate (except for a few small quirks in Maine and Nebraska). Under this winner-take-all method, it does not matter what percentage of citizens voted for the alternative candidate. For example, during the 2016 election, more than four million people voted for Donald Trump in California; but, because the majority still voted for Hillary Clinton (around eight million), all fifty-five electoral votes in California went to Clinton. Trump's literal millions of votes in California were effectively useless.

Thus, when citizens vote for a presidential candidate, what they are actually voting for is who their state electoral delegates will vote for. Although the citizens vote for the president in November, the electoral delegates meet in mid-December to formally cast *their* votes and actually elect the next president.

Sometimes, however, these electoral delegates vote against the results of their state's popular vote. These delegates have been dubbed "faithless electors," and there have been around one hundred instances of such faithlessness in modern history. The 2016 election of President Donald Trump saw an unusually high number of faithless electors, with ten instances in total. In the State of Washington, four delegates cast votes for individuals other than Hillary Clinton, who won the state. In Hawaii, one delegate also refused to vote for Clinton. In Texas, two delegates refused to vote for Donald Trump. Today, most states have laws that subject faithless electors to fines or imprisonment (although this doesn't necessarily negate their vote). Washington became the most recent state to pass such a law in the wake of their four electoral delegates going rogue in 2016. A few states also have laws that simply void any faithless votes from electoral delegates. Nevertheless, around one dozen states still have no laws or enforcement mechanisms to ensure that electoral delegates vote for their state's chosen candidate. Technically, electoral delegates in these states are free to completely upend the presidential election.

The Path to the Presidency

Although the District of Columbia has no full membership in Congress, the territory is allotted three electoral votes of its own, making 538 total electoral votes available. The presidential candidate who secures 270 of those votes is automatically the winner of the election. This is why the presidential election is sometimes referred to as "The Race to 270." For those of you who are math-challenged (just like most lawyers), 538 divided in half is 269, making 270 the majority of electoral votes.

Here, we find our first source of controversy with the Electoral College. That is, the popular vote does not matter at all. Indeed, it is wholly irrelevant if the majority of the country votes overwhelmingly for one candidate. All that matters is the magic number of 270 electoral votes. Although it is relatively rare, the elections of 1876, 1888, 2000, and 2016 produced an Electoral College winner who actually lost the popular vote. In President Trump's victory of 2016, he secured a whopping 304 electoral votes, but still lost the popular count by nearly three million votes.

How is this possible?

There are two main factors that explain how a candidate can lose the popular vote but still win the Electoral College. First, remember that each state uses a winner-take-all approach with their electoral votes. This means that a candidate who secures 99 percent of the vote in a state will get the same number of electoral votes as one who secures only 51 percent. Now, consider very populated states such as California and New York. In the 2016 election, Hillary Clinton secured four million more votes than Donald Trump in California, and two million more in New York. Indeed, Clinton won by sweeping margins in both states; by contrast, Trump won his "large" states, Florida and Texas, by much closer margins. In fact, Trump won Florida by only around one hundred thousand votes. Despite this razor-thin margin, he still walked away with all of Florida's twenty-nine electoral votes. Overall, while Trump won more states than Clinton, he generally did so by much smaller margins, which allowed Clinton to keep accumulating popular votes, in addition to her landslide wins in huge states like California and New York.

Second, remember that all states, no matter how small, will receive at least three electoral votes. Alaska, Montana, North Dakota, South Dakota, and Wyoming all have three electoral votes. In the 2016 election, Trump won each of these states and tallied up fifteen electoral votes without gaining much in the way of popular vote numbers. In fact, in Wyoming, only 250,000 people in the entire state cast a vote. This makes sense when you consider that the entire state only has a population of around 575,000, which is about the size of Albuquerque, New Mexico.

Okay, let's pause for a moment. It's finally time to do it: for the first time in history, someone needs to talk about Wyoming.

Because Wyoming is the least populated state in the country and yet still has three electoral votes, a citizen's single vote in this state carries more influence than anywhere else. Think of it this way: with roughly 575,000 people in the state, and three electoral votes at stake, each electoral vote represents around 190,000 people. Now, compare this with California, the state with the largest population. With nearly 40,000,000 people in the state and 55 electoral votes, each electoral vote represents around 725,000 people. Thus, an individual's vote in Wyoming carries about four times more influence than a vote in California.

For many, such disparate influence is a major problem. Opponents argue that a citizen's vote should not wield less influence simply because their state is more populous than another. The Electoral College, by design, is antithetical to the notion of one person, one vote. As a particular point of contention, many of the smaller states with a larger influence per vote happen to have mostly white populations, whereas larger states with "diluted" votes tend to be more racially diverse.

Swing States

You have likely heard of the term "swing state." Swing states are those states that, based on polls and statistics, have an almost equally reasonable chance of being won by either presidential candidate. The margins in these states are often extremely narrow. Because of the Electoral College, swing states end up being where all of the action takes place.

The unique importance of swing states is once again a result of the winner-take-all approach each state uses when awarding their electoral votes. Both the Democratic and Republican parties have developed solid bases of support in particular states that are practically guaranteed to vote for their candidate in a presidential election. Alabama is almost certainly going to vote for the Republican candidate, whereas Oregon will almost certainly vote for the Democrat. Thus, presidential candidates need not spend any considerable time campaigning in these states. For example, once Hillary Clinton secured the Democratic nomination during the 2016 election, she never again visited California as part of her campaign—there was simply no need. Cultivating another one million votes in the state with a hard-hitting series of campaign activities would not have afforded her any more electoral votes. By contrast, Florida, which is a large swing state, was visited by both candidates more than thirty times. During each presidential election, candidates typically ignore the non-competitive states and instead pour their finite resources into the few swing states. This is simply the best strategy for reaching the magical number of 270.

Many opponents of the Electoral College also find the emphasis on swing states (dubbed the "swing state privilege") to be problematic. Because so much effort is devoted to these states, more attention is paid to their specific problems and needs. Presidential candidates will often campaign by making promises explicitly to swing states. For example, auto manufacturing is a large component of the economy in Michigan (a swing state). During the 2016 election, both Trump and Clinton made campaign promises to help bolster the auto industry job market in Michigan. At the same time, both candidates pledged to help mitigate the Flint water crisis. To be sure, no such promises were made for the job markets or ecological problems faced in non-swing states like Mississippi or New Jersey.

But . . . Why?

Let's take a look at how our presidential elections ended up being decided by the Electoral College system.

During the summer of 1787, the Constitutional Convention took place in Philadelphia. There, our Founding Fathers got together and attempted to hammer out the details regarding how our country was to be governed. Among the details to be discussed was the question of how our nation would elect its chief leader. It's important to remember that our Founding Fathers were colonists fleeing a tyrannical monarchy in England. Seeking to improve upon the troubles of their former country, significant effort was paid toward avoiding any system in which one individual could amass too much power. Several ideas were proposed, with three given the most attention.

The first idea was to allow Congress to pick the president. However, this idea was rejected due to concerns that it would threaten the separation of powers. The first three articles of the Constitution mandate that the federal government be split into three branches of power: the executive branch (the president), the legislative branch (Congress), and the judicial branch (the courts). Separating power in this way allowed for an important system of checks and balances. However, if Congress were responsible for electing the president, improprieties could arise and cause the balance of power to shift too strongly toward the legislative branch.

The second idea was to allow the legislatures of each state to elect the president. This idea was rejected over concerns that states would purposely select a weak president in order to increase their own power. Remember, the United States operates under the principle of federalism, with two autonomous governing bodies operating simultaneously (the states and the federal government). Allowing state government leaders to elect the leader of the federal government could threaten federalist principles.

Finally, the third idea was a national popular election. This idea was rejected for a variety of reasons. Chief among those was the concern that American citizens strewn across a vast and developing nation would not possess sufficient knowledge to make informed choices about presidential candidates. As declared (a bit harshly) by George Mason, "It would be as unnatural to refer the choice of a proper candidate for chief Magistrate to the people, as it would be to refer a trial of colours to a blind man." Others feared that harmful foreign influence and disinformation could more readily reach the average voter. Notably, the southern states were also particularly opposed to the popular vote due to the fact that a significant proportion of their population (enslaved people) could not legally vote. This particular "issue" was ultimately resolved in the infamous Three-Fifths Compromise, in which all enslaved individuals were to be counted as three-fifths of a free person for the purposes of calculating state representation.

Even after vigorous debates, the issue of the presidential election initially went unresolved. In order to arrive at a final resolution on this question and a few lingering others, the Grand Committee on Postponed Questions was formed (fantastic name, right?). Although it is not certain who actually first envisioned the idea, the Committee ultimately proposed the Electoral College, which was later written into Article II, Section 1 of the Constitution.

Recent Gallup polls from 2020 show that the majority of the population (around 61 percent) supports the abolishment of the Electoral College in favor of a national popular vote. That said, many legal scholars do laud the system. According to its proponents, the Electoral College reflects the inherent compromise that built our nation. Since its inception, our country has had to work to balance the interests of small states versus large states. As an example, consider how each state, no matter its size, is allotted two senators. At the time of its founding, many feared the dominance that the then-populous states of New York, Pennsylvania, and Virginia would have over each election. Today, the Electoral College continues to protect against the same concern. Without it, many fear that politicians would simply target dense metropolitan areas along the coastlines without ever so much as paying a nod to the numerous states existing in "flyover country." As a point of reference, there are 3,143 counties in the United States, but more than half of the entire population lives in only 143 of them. By giving each individual state a share of electoral votes, presidential candidates are more likely to win by building broad support that spans the country, rather than only a few populated pockets.

In any case, love it or hate it, the system is unlikely to change anytime soon. To abolish the Electoral College, Congress would need to pass a constitutional amendment, which requires approval from two-thirds of Congress, plus ratification from three-fourths of the states. Alternatively, a new constitutional convention could be convened if requested by at least two-thirds of the states, which is something that's never actually happened since our nation's inception. Either method is unlikely to prove successful. Recall that numerous smaller states benefit immensely from the Electoral College, as well as the several swing states. It is doubtful that such states would choose to diminish the power they currently enjoy.

SECTION 5: EMPLOYERS AND LANDLORDS

If You Punch a Guy in the Face at Work, It's Probably Your Employer's Fault

Respondeat Superior

Respondeat superior! Sounds like something Harry Potter might yell at a dementor. The phrase (like most legal terms) is derived from Latin and translates literally to "let the master answer."

Respondeat superior is another type of legal liability. This time, it's *vicarious* liability, which basically just means that someone is liable for the harm caused by someone else. Vicarious liability applies in several situations. For example, parents are typically vicariously liable for any harm their children cause. If a small child were to push an old man to the ground and break his hip, the child's parents—obviously not the child—would be legally on the hook to pay for the man's medical bills and other damages. Until the 1950s, some state laws made a husband vicariously liable for any harm caused by his wife, even if the harm took place outside of his presence and had nothing to do with him.

Respondeat superior refers to the specific type of vicarious liability that makes an employer liable for the harm caused by their employees. It's the general rule across the country that if an employee causes harm to someone (or engages in a "wrongful act," as the courts like to say), the employer can be sued and held responsible, even if the employer had absolutely nothing to do with it.

However, there are a few ground rules. For example, an employee must generally commit the wrongful act while doing some kind of work for the employer. Courts refer to this as the employee being within the "scope of work." The work being done doesn't necessarily need to be in response to a specific order from the boss—the employee just needs to be performing some kind of work. A good litmus test for this is to ask: was the employee on the clock? If so, this usually (but not always!) means the employer will be liable for the employee's wrongful acts.

A common example of *respondeat superior* liability can be found in car wrecks. Indeed, employers face immense liability when their employees drive as part of their job. Imagine a small mom and pop pizza shop. The owners are struggling to get by. Poor Mr. Albertelli spends sleepless nights wondering why people don't buy his pizza. It's great pizza, but they don't have the money to advertise, and the local chains can always undercut their prices. Mrs. Albertelli, ever the innovator, has the idea to attract more customers with a delivery service. They manage to scrounge up just enough funds to hire an eighteen-year-old boy, Kevin, at minimum wage. "The tips will be good," poor Mr. Albertelli tells Kevin, wishing he could offer him a better wage. His very first night on the job, Kevin, while blasting Hanson's "MMMbop" on the radio and texting his girlfriend Clarice, negligently runs a red light and T-bones a mother and daughter. Both are seriously injured. Knowing Kevin has no money, the mother sues the Albertellis for every dime they've ever made and will ever make. Under the doctrine of *respondeat superior*, the Albertellis are liable for the car wreck.

Now, let's use these same characters to illustrate when *respondeat superior* does *not* apply. Suppose Kevin has just dropped off a pizza to a local customer. On his way back to the shop, he gets a text from Clarice asking him to come over. Kevin knows there are more pizzas waiting for him at the shop, but he decides that he can spare a few minutes with Clarice and starts driving to her house. About halfway there, he again runs a red light and T-bones the mother and daughter. In this case, the Albertellis would not be responsible for the wreck, because Kevin had gone on what is called a "frolic." Where an employee abandons the employer's business objectives and pursues personal interests, even while still on the clock, the employer is no longer liable for the employee. In most states, employers also aren't liable for employees when they are driving to and from work, or to and from lunch breaks.

CRASH COURSE

Vicarious liability is inherently tied to the topic of tort law. Before anyone gets too excited, tort law has absolutely nothing to do with delicious chocolate tortes. Rather, torts are an important aspect of civil law. In fact, in law schools throughout the United States, tort law is one of the foundational courses required during the first-year curriculum, along with criminal law, civil law, contract law, constitutional law, and property law.

So, what are torts?

Generally speaking, a tort is an act or omission that causes some kind of injury or harm. Importantly, torts are *civil* offenses, not criminal, although the same act can be both a tort and a crime (for example, battery is both a criminal offense and a tort). Victims of torts sue the offender in civil court and, if they win their case, most often receive financial compensation. The ultimate purpose of tort law is to compensate the victim for the harms they have suffered.

Most torts can be separated into two camps: negligent and intentional. Let's discuss each in turn.

Negligence

Acting negligently, and subsequently causing harm to someone, is a tort. Virtually any act or omission can give rise to tort liability, so long as it is done negligently. The opportunities here are truly limitless; cases of negligence can involve anything from the accidental discharge of improperly stored fireworks to a wet floor that causes someone to slip and fall.

Put very simply, the concept of negligence in tort law can be thought of as carelessness. It is a failure to act with the level of care that a reasonable person would have exercised under the same circumstances. Similar to self-defense, the "reasonable person" standard largely controls negligence cases.

Personal injury lawsuits, something that everyone has heard of before, almost always involve negligence of some kind. As our society has grown more litigious, personal injury lawsuits have become their own specialized area of the law, with some lawyers labeling themselves explicitly as "personal injury attorneys." These attorneys will find a plaintiff who has suffered a harm and make the case that a particular defendant acted negligently to cause the harm. If successful, their client will reap a financial reward. Personal injury attorneys almost always work on a "contingency fee" basis, meaning that the lawyer works in return for a percentage of the financial reward the client receives (most often 30 percent). Under this arrangement, the lawyer only gets paid if their client is awarded money (whether via settlement or court award).

Common personal injury lawsuits derive from incidents like car accidents, slip and fall injuries, workplace injuries, injuries from defective products, dog bites (another area of vicarious liability), and medical malpractice.

One of the earliest personal injury cases in written record occurred in 1923 in <u>Donoghue v. Stevenson</u>. The case actually took place in Scotland, but its decision went on to influence the law in the United States. Donoghue was drinking a bottle of ginger beer in a café located in the small village of Paisley. Unbeknownst to her, a decomposed snail was inside the bottle. She only noticed the snail after already drinking a substantial amount of the beer. Donoghue allegedly suffered significant gastrointestinal illness from the snail and sued the manufacturer of the beer, Stevenson. The court ultimately ruled in favor of Donoghue, finding that Stevenson had been negligent to allow a snail to enter into his manufacturing process. Today, it might seem unsurprising that Donoghue prevailed in her claim—after all, if you became sick after finding a decomposing snail inside any of your food products or beverages, your first thought might be to call a lawyer. Prior to the early twentieth century, however, personal injury cases were extremely rare. <u>Donoghue v. Stevenson</u> is credited with opening the floodgates for these sorts of claims to proliferate.

Intentional Torts

In addition to negligence, some torts can be intentional. As it sounds, an intentional tort occurs when someone intentionally engages in an act or omission that causes some kind of injury or harm, as opposed to negligently doing so. For example, a car accident is often the result of negligence. However, if a person intentionally hits you with their car and causes you injury, then the intentional tort of battery has occurred.

There are several common types of intentional torts, such as defamation, false imprisonment, assault, battery, and the intentional infliction of emotional distress.

Defamation usually involves intentionally making a false statement that damages the reputation of someone (the "harm" suffered here is the damaged reputation). To get specific, "libel" is a defamatory statement that is written, whereas "slander" is a defamatory statement that is spoken.

False imprisonment occurs when someone intentionally restricts another person's freedom of movement, such as during a kidnapping or sexual assault (the harm here can be either psychological trauma or physical injury). A shopkeeper who abuses their privilege to detain a suspected shoplifter might end up committing the tort of false imprisonment.

Assault and battery are closely related, yet distinct. Interestingly, the common understanding of these words doesn't quite match with their legal definitions. Legally speaking, an assault is an intentional act that places another person in reasonable fear of harm, whether or not harm actually occurs. Battery, on the other hand, is the actual physical contact with someone that causes harm. Most people would think that to "assault" someone means to physically attack them. Technically, however, this would be more correctly described as a battery. That said, lawyers will often use the terms interchangeably in the spirit of easy understanding (this book has even done so). The terms "assault and battery" are also sometimes combined because a physical attack usually involves at first the fear of contact, followed by the actual contact itself.

The intentional infliction of emotional distress (IIED) is a particularly interesting tort. It occurs when someone intentionally engages in conduct that causes someone to experience severe emotional distress. In other words, making someone super upset is a legitimate tort, and you can be sued for it. One notable example of IIED occurred in 2016, when Terry Bollea (aka Hulk Hogan) sued Gawker Media after they released a sex tape of him. The jury found in favor of Bollea and awarded him more than $140,000,000.

Intentional Wrongful Acts (aka Intentional Torts)

Thus far, we've discussed an employer's liability for their employee's negligence, specifically running a red light while looking at a cellphone. Surprising to most, employers can also be liable when their employees commit intentional torts. This holds true even when these torts are egregious and violent acts.

Employer liability for intentional torts is a highly controversial issue. Remember, employers are only supposed to be liable for acts of their employees while in the scope of work. How, then, can intentional torts like battery possibly give rise to employer liability? Seldom, if ever, does a job include committing violent acts as part of its scope of work. Just as we saw with the Commerce Clause, the answer lies in extraordinarily broad judicial interpretation. Specifically, some courts have interpreted the meaning of "scope of work" to include any action that is "foreseeably related" to an employee's work.

Consider the following classic hypothetical introduced to virtually every first-year law student: a bouncer at a bar attempts to remove a rowdy customer but uses excessive force, punching the patron in the face and breaking his jaw. Is the bar owner liable? Yes. Although the bouncer committed an intentional tort (i.e., battery), his actions are still likely to be perceived by a court as foreseeably related to his employment. After all, physical and hostile contact with patrons is part of the bouncer's job and it is foreseeable that a hot-headed moment of excessive force could occur.

By contrast, what if the nightly DJ employed by the bar roughed up a customer in the same way? In this case, the bar owner would likely not be liable, because the DJ's job of playing music is completely unrelated to using physical force against patrons.

Being an Employer in California

One unique aspect of the California legal system is the state's relatively harsh stance against employers. Ask anyone who owns a business in California and they'll likely talk your ear off about the numerous hoops the state requires them to jump through. Indeed, it is an accepted fact in the legal community that California employment laws place the greatest burden upon employers compared to any other state.

In contrast, other states, like Delaware, tend to favor the company and employer. This is part of the reason why so many businesses are incorporated in Delaware. When a company incorporates within a state, it can generally (but not always) subject themselves to the laws of that state. In other words, if they are facing a lawsuit, they can demand that the laws of their state of incorporation apply during the case. As we have discussed, different states can have wildly different laws, which can make or break most legal disputes. All of the big businesses with smarty pants lawyers and executives want to reap the benefits of Delaware's employer-friendly laws, taxes, and courts. Go ahead and think of any big business. Odds are good that they're incorporated in Delaware.

Apple? Delaware.

Facebook? Delaware.

Google? Delaware.

Ford? Delaware.

Coca Cola? Delaware.

Boeing? Delaware.

General Electric? Delaware.

Tesla? Delaware.

You get the point.

With regard to the doctrine of *respondeat superior*, California courts have stretched the concept of "scope of work" to perhaps the most expansive view in the country, finding employers liable for some highly questionable acts.

In <u>Rodgers v. Kemper Constr. Co.</u>, two men, Herd and O'Brien, both employees of Kemper Construction Company, had finished up their shift at a large jobsite. Done with work, the two men changed into their personal clothes and drank several beers in a locker room on the jobsite. After finishing their drinks, they started to work on O'Brien's pickup truck in the parking lot. A few hours later, wanting their drunken fun to continue, Herd and O'Brien set out on foot across the jobsite to look for another coworker who owed them money. They planned to use the money to continue drinking at a bar in town. The jobsite was large and the walk long, but soon they happened upon an employee from a different company who was operating a bulldozer. Herd and O'Brien asked the bulldozer operator, Rodgers, for a ride across the jobsite. Rodgers refused, explaining that it was against his company's policies. Apparently dissatisfied with this response, Herd and O'Brien began to beat Rodgers, pummeling him with their fists and some nearby rocks before taking off on foot back to the parking lot. Injured, Rodgers drove the bulldozer to where his supervisor was working. Rodgers and the supervisor then proceeded to the parking lot, where they saw Herd and O'Brien. Once again, Herd and O'Brien began fighting with Rodgers. During this scuffle, poor Rodgers was hit from behind, rendering him unconscious.

Rodgers sustained multiple serious injuries and sued Kemper Construction Company. The court found that Herd and O'Brien were within their scope of work while attacking Rodgers, and therefore

Kemper was liable. The court offered two main rationales for their conclusion. First, the court reasoned that it was "conceivably" a benefit for Kemper that Herd and O'Brien remained on the premises after-hours. Even if they were drunk, the court made the argument that Kemper could have still utilized their services in the event that an unexpected work need arose. Second, the court tapped into some psychological theory and suggested that, by putting men together on a jobsite, "normal human traits" are to be expected, which include emotional flare-ups and violence. As a result of this male proclivity for aggression, it was foreseeable that fights would ensue on a jobsite.

Recapitulating for a moment, this California court found that an employer should be liable for their employees' drunken brawl, even though the brawl occurred after the work shift had ended and was catalyzed by the employees trying to get an unauthorized ride on a bulldozer across the jobsite to find money for more booze. Shocking many across the legal community, the Court found that these actions were sufficiently within their scope of work, such that the company was on the hook for the harm they caused. At trial, Rodgers was ultimately awarded more than one million dollars in today's dollars.

In Mary M. v. City of Los Angeles, the California Supreme Court found the City of Los Angeles vicariously liable for the rape committed by one of its on-duty police officers. At around 2:30 a.m., the plaintiff ("Mary") was driving home alone when Sergeant Leigh Schroyer of the LAPD stopped her for erratic driving. Mary failed a field sobriety test, but instead of taking her to jail, Schroyer drove her to her home. After entering her house, he told her that he expected "payment" for not charging her with driving under the influence. Mary tried to run away, but Schroyer grabbed her, threw her on the couch, and raped her.

Generally, and in most states other than California, an employer can never be held liable for the sexual misconduct of an employee because such conduct is, by definition, outside the scope of employment. One judge reduced this idea to a very simple point, explaining, "No one is ever hired to commit sexual torts against others." Nevertheless, much like the Rodgers v. Kemper case above, the California court in this case also decided to focus on the concept of foreseeability, specifically the foreseeability of sexual misconduct in the line of police work. The court noted that police officers have the authority to detain citizens and touch them without consent. Highlighting this unique authority, the court determined it was foreseeable that police officers would abuse it for personal gain. Thus, the court found that Schroyer's rape was related enough to his employment that the City of Los Angeles (Schroyer's employer) was liable for it. The plaintiff was awarded around $700,000 in today's dollars at trial.

But . . . Why?

Nobody wants to face a hefty lawsuit for conduct that someone else committed. Any employer facing a lawsuit under *respondeat superior* is going to feel as if the legal world has conspired against them.

While seemingly unfair to the individual employer, lawmakers have determined that, as a matter of general social policy, employers are better positioned to compensate victims than the employees who ultimately caused the harm. This is because employers can cushion themselves against this potential liability by purchasing liability insurance. This, in turn, results in the employer charging slightly higher prices for their products or services in order to pay for the insurance. In this way, *respondeat superior* liability can be passed off as merely another cost of doing business.

Think back to the scalding hot McDonald's coffee in the case of Stella Liebeck. Imagine that a minimum-wage employee at McDonald's becomes irate with a recalcitrant patron. Bitter words are exchanged, and the employee ends up tossing a cup of this scalding-hot coffee into the face of the patron, resulting in excessive burns and millions of dollars in medical costs. The employee has no real assets: she owns no home and has only $1,500 in her bank account. McDonald's, on the other hand, has *slightly* deeper pockets, with revenues per year in excess of twenty billion dollars. The only one who could actually afford to cover the victim's medical expenses is McDonald's. And McDonald's, as the argument would go, can protect against this type of cost by purchasing liability insurance. To pay for the liability insurance, McDonald's would increase the price of an order of french fries by a cent or two, placing the actual cost of this liability upon society as a whole (or at least french fry eaters). Legal scholars refer to this concept as effectively "spreading the risk" of legal liability.

CRASH COURSE

Let's now jump into a particularly hot legal topic with massive implications involving employment law: independent contractors in the ride-sharing sector.

Independent Contractors

All of the drivers for the ride-sharing behemoths, Uber and Lyft, are not actually employees of those companies. Instead, they are independent contractors (let's call them "ICs").

Employers love to hire ICs in lieu of regular employees. Why? For one thing, they cut costs. Although ICs sometimes charge more per hour than an employee might regularly be paid (because ICs work "on demand" and often have specialized skills), they are usually, overall, a much cheaper option for employers. Numerous costs are associated with hiring and paying an employee above and beyond the employee's actual wage or salary. Employers must make several required payments on behalf of their employees, such as contributions into Social Security and Medicare, unemployment insurance, and workers' compensation insurance. These additional and legally required contributions from the employer often increase overall payroll costs by up to 30 percent beyond the wage or salary itself. This all goes without even mentioning the large amount of time and money spent onboarding new employees into a company. None of these extra costs are required when hiring ICs.

But employers also love ICs because they reduce exposure to legal liability. Employees have a wide array of rights under state and federal laws; if any of these numerous rights are violated, they can form the basis for a potential lawsuit against an employer. Because ICs are considered separate and distinct entities from the company, they are not entitled to the same rights as regular employees. For example, ICs generally have no right to:

- be paid at the minimum wage and/or receive overtime;

- be protected against employment discrimination;

- form a union; or

- take paid take maternity leave, sick leave, or vacation.

Beyond all this, there's one other sneaky legal reason why employers—particularly employers in the ride-sharing business—want desperately to hire exclusively independent contractors as their drivers. Can you guess why? Think back to the most common example of *respondeat superior* liability.

That's right: car wrecks. Uber alone has given passengers more than three billion rides.

There is no clear data showing just how many car wrecks Uber drivers have been involved in, but you can bet it's a substantial amount. If even a tiny fraction of those accidents resulted in lawsuits against Uber, the company likely wouldn't be able to survive financially. Luckily for ride-sharing companies, wrongful acts committed by ICs generally will not subject an employer to *respondeat superior* liability, even if the IC is within their scope of work. So, if Kevin is now working for Uber as an IC and T-bones the same mother and daughter after running a red light, Uber generally won't be liable. In order to help compensate potential car accident victims, many states have passed laws requiring ride-share drivers to carry large insurance policies with at least a one-million-dollar limit.

Currently, several states are in the process of passing laws that make it more difficult for employers, such as Uber, Lyft, and other "gig economy" companies (DoorDash, Postmates, Seamless, etc.), to classify workers as ICs instead of regular employees. The purpose of such laws is to protect workers from being denied important benefits like health insurance and a minimum wage by being purposefully classified as an IC. For example, many ride-share workers can end up making below minimum wage after tallying up the fares they receive and the hours they work (not to mention personal expenses such as gas, vehicle maintenance, and auto insurance). Unsurprisingly, gig economy companies have spent hundreds of millions of dollars lobbying against these new laws. According to their calculations, classifying workers as employees would lead to mass layoffs, or perhaps even bankruptcies. Additionally, the traditional freedoms enjoyed by ICs, such as making their own schedules and having minimum supervision, might disappear if companies are forced to start treating them, accounting for them, and paying them as regular employees.

The law is struggling to adapt to the role of ICs in these new technology-based spheres of work. Frankly, many state legislatures appear a bit confused by which course of action is ultimately correct. California, for example, passed its controversial "AB-5" law in 2019, which required most independent contractors in the gig economy to be reclassified as employees. However, just a few months later, Proposition 22 was passed, which promptly reversed course and allowed gig economy workers to remain independent contractors. Over the next several years, this area of law is likely to keep experiencing twists and turns as states wrestle with what is best for their workers.

The Police Have No Duty to Protect You, but Landlords Do
The Warranty of Habitability

In November of 1966, Sarah Kline sustained serious injuries after being robbed and attacked in the common hallway of her apartment complex. When Kline first moved into the apartment several years earlier, the landlord employed a doorman service to supervise the front door twenty hours per day. However, by the time Kline was attacked, the landlord had removed the doorman service.

Kline was not the first tenant to be attacked inside the apartment complex. Two months prior, another woman, Leona Sullivan, had been attacked in a nearly identical fashion in the very same hallway. Crime rates in the area were on the rise, and the landlord had been notified of the increasing number of robberies, burglaries, and attacks throughout the apartment complex. Kline herself urged the landlord to take additional steps to secure the building. And yet, the landlord did nothing.

Following the attack, Kline sued the landlord for failing to protect her. In Kline v. 1500 Massachusetts Avenue Apartment Corp., the court reached the groundbreaking decision that the landlord had a duty to protect his tenants, and that he had failed to do so. As you may recall, an individual generally does not have a duty to protect someone else, unless a special relationship exists. Prior to Kline, landlords were not thought of as having a special relationship with their tenants, and thus had no legal duty to protect them. The Kline decision catalyzed a trend across the country of courts finding landlords liable for failing to adequately protect their tenants, a trend that continues today.

The rationale behind the Kline decision was fairly straightforward: The law typically imputes a special relationship where one party has some kind of control over another. As the owners of the property in which the tenants reside, landlords are ultimately in control of securing tenant safety. If a security service is to be hired, new locks installed, or a broken window repaired, it is the landlord who has the control to undertake these activities. In fact, many apartment leases explicitly forbid tenants from making any changes to the property, such as adding additional door locks or installing bars on a window.

Of course, the ruling in Kline did not imply that landlords are liable for *every* crime that takes place on their property (i.e., they are not strictly liable). Rather, the landlord's duty to protect is based on what is reasonable given a property's specific circumstances. Put another way, a landlord must act negligently in order to fail in their duty to protect. In Kline, the landlord's negligence was clear: he was aware that violent attacks were frequently occurring in the apartment complex and yet failed to take any action. In fact, he terminated the service of the doorman, one of the few safety precautions that had been in place.

Another example of a landlord failing to protect a tenant occurred in the tragic case of Vasquez v. Residential Investments, Inc. Here, a woman was stabbed to death inside her apartment by a jealous ex-boyfriend. The ex-boyfriend gained entry into the unit by sticking his hand through a missing glass pane in the front door and opening the door from the outside. The woman had been reporting the missing glass in the door to the landlord for several weeks. Each time she reported the issue, she expressed her safety concerns. The landlord was found to be negligent in omitting to fix the missing glass, and thus failed in his duty to protect the woman.

Importantly, a landlord's duty to protect reaches beyond adequately securing the property from criminal acts. Landlords also have a duty to protect tenants from preventable accidents caused by defects on the property. Injuries arising from slippery walkways, broken steps, open trenches, broken hot water faucets, or virtually any other defect can result in a landlord being held liable. Again, however, landlords are not strictly liable for all accidents that occur on their property; negligence on the part of the landlord is required. Landlords are most commonly found negligent when they have knowledge of a dangerous defect but don't repair it in a timely manner, or fail to take extra safety precautions until the repair is complete.

It might be surprising to learn that landlords have a duty to protect tenants, but police don't have a duty to protect citizens. Alternatively, for some of you, the control rationale offered in Kline might justify holding police and landlords to different standards. After all, it is perhaps a fair argument that landlords have more intimate and immediate control over their tenants' safety than a police officer does over an average citizen. Another point to consider is that landlords, just like employers, are typically business entities that can buffer themselves from liability by purchasing insurance. The price of this insurance is offset in the form of slightly higher rents, a burden borne by society as a whole. By contrast, police officers are individuals who do not charge fees for their services, and thus cannot so easily cover their personal liabilities with insurance (although some states, like New York and Colorado, are currently considering the idea). As a general trend, the law is more keen to impose liability upon those who can protect themselves with insurance. Nothing provides job security to insurance agents quite like the legal system!

The Warranty of Habitability

In addition to their duty to protect, landlords have another very important responsibility: the warranty of habitability. This warranty is a legal doctrine that requires landlords to keep their property in "habitable" (i.e., satisfactory) living condition. Notably, the warranty is legally implied in every rental agreement, which means it always exists, even if a lease does not make any explicit warranties about living condition or promises to make repairs.

The doctrine stems from the landmark 1970 case of Javins v. First National Realty Corp. Ethel Javins and her two roommates refused to pay rent due to the very poor living conditions of their apartment. When the landlord sued to evict them, the tenants introduced evidence at trial showing that the apartment suffered from dozens of plumbing, electrical, and fire code violations, and was also filled with mouse feces, dead mice, and roaches. The court ruled that the landlord had an obligation to keep the apartment in a sufficiently habitable condition, and that such an obligation was always implied between landlords and their tenants, even if not included in the lease, as explained by the court:

"When American city dwellers, both rich and poor, seek 'shelter' today, they seek a well-known package of goods and services—a package which includes not merely walls and ceilings, but also adequate heat, light and ventilation, serviceable plumbing facilities, secure windows and doors, proper sanitation, and proper maintenance."

The Javins ruling was a striking development in landlord-tenant law, which previously viewed landlords as having no duty to keep a property in a certain condition or to make repairs unless explicitly contracted for in a lease. Indeed, it is difficult to over-emphasize the scope of legal reform triggered by the ruling; the case catalyzed a fundamentally different set of responsibilities owed between a landlord and tenant. Today, every state (except Arkansas) has its own version of the warranty of habitability, and a breach of the warranty usually means that a tenant does not have to pay rent until conditions in the apartment are made habitable.

In most states, statutes and various building codes set out the specific definitions of what it actually means to be "habitable." In typical progressive fashion, California has taken the lead in crafting one of the most expansive statutes enumerating numerous standards that, if violated, constitute a breach of the warranty of habitability. Specifically, California Civil Code Section 1941.1 requires landlords to provide everything from an adequate number of trashcans to working telephone jacks and electrical outlets.

As many states have expanded their warranty of habitability laws, the doctrine has become a source of controversy. Supporters argue that it protects impoverished tenants from abusive landlords, which is particularly important given that landlords generally have much more power than tenants. For example, when involved in legal disputes, statistics show that around 95 percent of landlords have legal representation, compared with only 5 percent of tenants. On the other hand, opponents claim that the warranty significantly drives up rental pricing, encourages landlords to abandon older buildings in disadvantaged communities, and turns landlords into *de facto* city building code inspectors.

CRASH COURSE

Security Deposits

For lawyers practicing in landlord-tenant law, by far the most common questions they receive from potential clients involve a landlord's alleged abuse of security deposit funds. A security deposit, as you likely already know, is a sum of money that a landlord takes from a tenant upfront that can be used later to cover unforeseen expenses caused by the tenant. Most often, these sorts of expenses include damage to the property, key replacements, cleaning, or unpaid rent. Legally, all security deposit funds not used for a proper purpose must be returned to the tenant at the end of the lease. The money belongs strictly to the tenant, only subject to landlord use for qualified reasons. Unfortunately, landlords have a notorious reputation for being less than scrupulous when returning security deposits.

I left my apartment completely spotless before moving out but the landlord kept $500 of the security deposit for "cleaning!" Sound familiar? Odds are good that you or one of your friends have experienced a situation similar to this.

According to most state laws, landlords can only use security deposit funds to cover a few specific categories: unpaid tenant bills (such as utilities), unpaid rent, penalties for breaking a lease early, replacing items (such as keys or parking gate clickers), cleaning, and damage to the unit. Importantly, the cleaning and damage categories have some unique restrictions. Security deposits cannot be used for damage that is part of the normal "wear and tear" during a lease. For example, things like faded paint, worn carpet, and minor dents or holes in a wall cannot be repaired using security deposit funds. Similarly, cleaning costs can only be covered by a security deposit if the tenant left the property in an excessively dirty condition (i.e., dirtier than when they received the unit).

Landlords must also clearly itemize each deduction they make from a security deposit and offer this list to the tenant. The security deposit itself, along with the list of any itemized deductions, must be returned to the tenant within a specified amount of time, usually between fourteen and thirty days after their lease expires, depending on the state.

Improperly withholding funds from a security deposit is categorically and indisputably illegal. Yet, landlords often fraudulently deduct expenses from security deposits or fail to return any portion of the deposit at all. Why? Well, the simple answer is that landlords usually aren't held accountable for security deposit fraud.

Here's the rub: most tenants have no idea how to dispute the return (or lack thereof) of their security deposit. The law on this issue can be nebulous and complex, and many people wouldn't even know how to start the dispute process. *Perhaps a lawyer will help me?* Doubtful. Most lawyers will not even consider taking on a new client unless their potential financial gain is at least a few thousand dollars. Security deposit disputes typically only involve between $500-$2000. That's a significant sum for most people, but not enough to entice a lawyer to take on the case. For those lawyers who are willing to help, average fees can range between $300-500 per hour, meaning that just a few hours of a lawyer's work will completely negate the benefit of getting the security deposit back (if your lawyer is even successful).

Landlords understand these irksome legal dynamics—that the financial harm suffered by tenants, while seriously aggravating, is usually not enough to persuade someone to help them. As such, they feel fairly confident in carrying on like the lords of their fiefdoms, fraudulently withholding funds from security deposits, knowing that their actions will likely go unrebuked.

For those who aren't willing to let such transgressions slide, the very best thing you can do is take extremely detailed photos before your move-in and after you leave, and also make a list of everything you were given during your move-in and everything you returned to the landlord. These photos and documents can then be used in small claims court, which is the topic of our next discussion.

There Is a Court System Where Lawyers Are Forbidden
Small Claims Court

Often referred to as the "People's Court," the small claims court champions equal and accessible justice perhaps more than any other aspect of our legal system. Here, the playing fields are leveled and the barriers to entry all but torn down; the little guy can take on the Fortune 500 company, the two neighbors can hash out their dispute over that barking dog, and the ambiguities in that contract you signed for the used car on Craigslist can finally get settled. It is a place where two parties, irrespective of sophistication or wealth, can state their claim before a government official capable of doling out justice. The therapeutic effect of simply having your case heard cannot be understated. And as it so happens, small claims court is also where the vast majority of all employer-employee and landlord-tenant legal disputes take place.

Recognizing the need for a streamlined court process where "minor" disputes could be adjudicated efficiently and expediently, Kansas created the first small claims court in 1912. Today, every state has created some form of a small claims court system.

The small claims system is not right for everyone. Small claims court is designed to only handle "minor" disputes, meaning that the amount of money involved in a dispute must be below a certain threshold. Most states cap claim limits somewhere between $2,500 and $10,000. The rationale here is that these relatively small disputes do not justify the use of the extremely complex and time-consuming "normal" court process.

In order to remain accessible to all citizens, traditional rules of evidence and procedure are significantly relaxed in small claims court. This is for good reason, as the amount of effort involved in introducing a single piece of evidence in a normal courtroom would make most people lash out in a horrid mixture of frustration and boredom. First, a proper foundation must be laid to demonstrate the relevance of the evidence; the evidence must be authenticated, marked correctly, and shown to the opposing side; and then the evidence must be presented to the judge using a ridiculous and archaic script. Fortunately, none of this is required in the small claims system. Parties to a dispute usually just bring copies of the relevant evidence, such as a contract or photograph, and hand it straight to the judge. Likewise, if witnesses are asked to testify (although this isn't very common), parties can question the witnesses without many limitations. Even hearsay testimony ("I heard from Bob that Amy defrauded Jim") is allowed in some states, despite it being strictly prohibited in all normal court proceedings.

Small claims court has no jury. Rather, the judge has the full authority to decide every aspect of the case. Importantly, judges in the small claims system typically take a more holistic approach to dispute resolution, listening to all of the available evidence and emphasizing conciliation and pragmatism over who is explicitly right or wrong. In this spirit, small claims courts are thought of as courts of "equity," which, at the risk of oversimplifying, just means that the judge has a very broad arsenal of remedies at their disposal: they can rescind or re-write a contract, decide themselves the value that something is worth, and order a party to stop doing something (e.g., blasting a stereo late at night) or keep doing something (e.g., finish painting that house). Overall, judges are going to do whatever makes the most sense for the specifics of a particular case, even if it means setting aside some legal formalities.

Although less formalistic, small claims court is still very much a genuine court, with serious real-world consequences. Judgments ren-dered in small claims court are official and fully enforceable. Just as in any other court, if the losing party fails to comply with the judgment, further actions can be taken, such as wage garnishment or placing liens on property.

Oddly enough, it was daytime television that largely popularized small claims court and brought its virtues into the national spotlight. Shows like *Judge Judy* became extremely popular in the late 1990s and early 2000s. In these shows, real-life small claim disputes were han-dled within a simulated courtroom set. Parties to the case signed con-tracts prior to the proceedings in which they agreed to be bound by the decisions made on the show. It bears mentioning that Judge Judy Sheindlin, aka Judge Judy, was a real judge with a very accomplished career prior to starring in her television show. Although her actions may have been a bit embellished and overly dramatic for the purpose of entertainment, the show did offer a glimpse into the relatively laid-back environment of small claims court, along with the kind of wacky controversies that sometimes take place there. For example, in one no-torious episode, a woman accused a man of stealing her wallet. Judge Judy's very first question asked the woman what was inside the wallet, to which she replied, "fifty dollars, some gift cards, earbuds, and a cal-culator." Suddenly, the man interjects and claims that there were no earbuds inside the wallet. *Yikes.* The case lasted twenty-six seconds, with Judge Judy (obviously) finding in favor of the woman and order-ing the man to pay her five hundred dollars.

How Small Claims Court Works

In a nutshell, pursuing a case in the small claims system involves five distinct steps:

Step 1 is to file the paperwork to begin the claim. Most often, plaintiffs will simply travel to their local county courthouse and find the small claims counter. The clerk will provide them with the necessary forms to fill out, which usually just include the plaintiff's name, the name of the defendant, the monetary amount in controversy, and a brief description of the dispute. Plaintiffs will also be required to pay the necessary court fees upfront (typically between twenty-five to one hundred dollars, depending on the court). Often, these fees will be included as part of the award at trial if the plaintiff wins.

Step 2 is to serve the defendant. This is by far the most complicated step of the process, and the place where plaintiffs are likely to make errors. For all official legal disputes, whether in small claims court or normal court, the defendant must be properly served. Being "served" simply means that the defendant is duly notified of the pending legal action. The law has always taken a very strict view on ensuring that defendants are notified well in advance of any lawsuit. All defendants are entitled to the opportunity to fully prepare for their case. It would be absurd to allow a plaintiff to surprise an unsuspecting defendant with a pending trial date and a text that reads, *Hey, I'm suing you, and by the way, trial is tomorrow. See ya' there.* This is particularly important given that defendants will often lose a case by default if they fail to show up without good reason.

To ensure that all defendants receive the required "service of process," as it is called, the law mandates that plaintiffs follow very specific rules when notifying the defendant (i.e., you can't just mail them a letter or tell them over the phone). Generally, a formal document must be presented to them by someone who is not a party to the lawsuit. Any person will do, even a friend or family member, so long as they are over eighteen years old and not actually involved in the case. The person who presents the document to the defendant must then submit an affidavit swearing that they delivered it to the correct person. In every case, a plaintiff must always properly serve the defendant before any trial can commence.

Sometimes, a would-be defendant knows that they have done something wrong and will try to avoid being served. As the logic goes,

If I can't be served, I can't be sued! In such situations, plaintiffs can hire professional process servers. These are companies that specialize in finding defendants and serving them. You may have seen this before on television shows or in movies—a calculating individual stalks the soon-to-be defendant and finally throws a pile of papers into their hands, announcing, "You've been served!"

Step 3 is to actually go to court. On the day of the trial, most small claims systems will first ask the parties if they want to try and resolve the dispute themselves with the assistance of a free mediator. If one or both parties refuse to mediate, the trial will commence. Both the plaintiff and defendant will have a chance to briefly explain their side of the case and offer any evidence. Witnesses may also be called at this time. However, witnesses must be subpoenaed several weeks before the trial, or voluntarily agree to show up. To subpoena a witness means to legally compel them to testify at the trial under the penalty of contempt of court. Much like properly serving a defendant, many strict rules must be followed to properly subpoena a witness.

Step 4 is to receive a ruling from the judge, and to have a judgment imposed on one of the parties. Most often, the judgment is in the form of money one party must pay to the other, although sometimes the judge may issue an "injunction," an order which commands a party to *stop* doing something, or "specific performance," which commands someone to *do* something, such as making good on a contract or completing a job.

Step 5, the final step, is the actual collection of the judgment ordered by the court. Many people don't realize this, but the court simply makes the judgment; it does not actually collect payment for you. Ideally, the losing party will simply comply with the judgment and life goes on. Other times, however, the judgment debtor (i.e., the loser) never actually pays out. In these situations, the prevailing party will have to return to court to get another court order to garnish the debtor's wages, or to put liens on their property.

Lawyers Stay Out!

Many lawyers tend to mock the small claims system. Often, it is looked down upon as the Pee Wee league of the legal system. This dismissive attitude is perhaps best addressed with one question: *Jealous, much?*

In many states, lawyers are strictly forbidden from representing any party at small claims court. Lawyers can advise a client before the trial and help them prepare, but they cannot actually advocate for them during the proceeding. Some courtrooms won't even allow lawyers to sit inside and observe. The rationale for this prohibition on attorneys is simple: they are too complicated. The purpose of the small claims system is to offer an accessible tribunal free from all of the confusion of normal court. Lawyers, with their near-super-human ability to needlessly overanalyze and overcomplicate, would most certainly muck up the process. Similarly, any party with a lawyer would be at a distinct advantage, which is not in the spirit of such an open-access tribunal. Even in states where lawyers are allowed, they are seldom present. The amount of money involved in a small claims dispute is, by definition, almost never large enough to justify the cost of a lawyer's fee.

Overall, for the unhappy tenant looking to get back her fraudulently withheld security deposit, or the disgruntled employee who was illegally denied his sick pay, small claims court is often the best avenue to seek legal redress. Even where some aspects can be a bit complicated, such as properly serving the defendant or subpoenaing a witness, most small claims systems have advisers who work free of charge to help guide parties through every step of the process.

SECTION 6: THE COURT SYSTEM

The Jury Selection Process Is Anything but Unbiased
Voir Dire

The jury is a paradox. Legal practitioners often laud the jury for its inherent wisdom and ability to seek the ultimate truth; but at the same time, attorneys also caution their clients, particularly during settlement negotiations and plea bargaining, to avoid juries like the plague. For many attorneys, presenting a case before a jury is like taking a plunge from an unknown height.

Consider the following real-world example with details that I have tweaked slightly for confidentiality reasons. A few years ago, I had a client (a corporation) that was defending against a lawsuit from an individual (the plaintiff) who alleged that the corporation's negligence had caused him to slip and fall while on their premises and suffer a traumatic brain injury. The injuries from the fall were actually very serious—he spent several months in the hospital and rehabilitation facilities, lost his ability to walk normally, and struggled with memory and complex speech. As is normal in such a case, several different medical experts offered their opinions on the plaintiff's level of injury, each with differing determinations. No expert could definitively state whether the plaintiff's injuries were permanent, or if they would resolve over time.

Part of my job was to research court cases with plaintiffs suffering similar brain injuries in order to determine how much financial compensation was typically awarded by the jury. I spent a full week researching over one hundred different cases, attempting to find those with fact patterns that most closely resembled ours. After my research had concluded, I wanted nothing more than to have that week of my life back. My research had accomplished nothing; it was an utterly useless waste of time. Jury awards in similar brain injury cases ranged from $200,000 to $20,000,000. The disparities were extraordinary, and there seemed to be no rhyme or reason for any of it.

The corporation was ultimately advised to settle the case to the tune of around $2,000,000. While that might seem like a hefty sum, it paled in comparison to the potential $20,000,000 payout that could have been awarded by a jury (not to mention the gigantic cost of attorney's fees incurred during trial). No one could be sure how this case's particular jury would react to this plaintiff's particular injuries, and the potential monetary risks involved were simply too high for the corporation not to settle.

As an additional example, consider one final time this book's favorite illustrative case of Stella Liebeck and the scalding McDonald's coffee. Initially following her injuries, Liebeck tried to settle the matter with McDonald's for $20,000. McDonald's countered by offering her a measly $800. After a court case was filed, but before the trial actually took place, Liebeck again tried to settle the matter, this time to the tune of $90,000, but McDonald's declined. Just days before the trial, Liebeck offered one last chance to McDonald's: $300,000. Again, McDonald's refused and decided to try their luck at trial. This turned out to be a grave mistake. The jury decided in favor of Liebeck and ultimately awarded her $2.86 million.

The fear of the jury's unpredictability is not unique to civil lawsuits; in fact, it is perhaps exacerbated in the criminal system where one's freedom, not just their bank account, is on the line. As we have discussed previously, around 95 percent of all criminal cases are resolved via plea bargains, not actual trials. The reasons offered for this extreme statistic are numerous, including overzealous prosecutors, under-enthused defense attorneys (public defenders appointed to those who cannot afford an attorney are often overworked and underpaid), and inherent biases in the justice system. While all of these critiques might be valid, most agree that the fear of the jury also plays a prominent role in avoiding criminal trials. Consider a situation in which a defendant is facing the threat of a federal criminal charge for the sale and distribution of ten grams of LSD. If convicted at trial, the defendant will face a mandatory minimum sentence of ten years in prison. Suppose now that the prosecutor offers a plea bargain deal in which the defendant only needs to plead guilty to the crime of simple possession, which typically carries a sentence of less than one year. Even if the defendant believes wholeheartedly that they are not guilty, the risk of the jury's unpredictable determination can be simply too much to bear.

Although we entrust juries with the decisive roles of determining truth and assessing guilt, and often refer to them as a hallmark of our democracy, our reverence is undercut by a sense of profound mistrust. In order to curb some of this mistrust, the law has reacted by strongly regulating the jury. Specifically, an extensive set of rules and procedures has been crafted to control who actually gets to sit on a jury. While the overarching aim of these rules is to select an unbiased and fair pool of jurors, their real-world application has led to some very questionable outcomes.

The History and Role of the Jury

Before getting into the process of selecting jurors, it's important to review a brief history of the jury and its role in our contemporary justice system. So strap in, we're getting historical.

The concept of juries dates as far back as ancient Greece. These earliest juries did not apply established law to situations, but rather heard arguments and made determinations based on general principles of fairness and justice (kind of similar to small claims judges). After the fall of the Roman empire, the Early Middle Ages saw little use of the jury, perhaps due to the frequent warfare and reduction in city-centric lifestyles.

For much of the Middle Ages, the Catholic Church dominated the Western legal system with its ecclesiastical (i.e., religion-focused) courts. Under this regime, judgments and punishments were often carried out through the "ordeal," a process by which an individual was accused of wrongdoing and then subjected to various divine tests. Supposedly, supernatural powers would benefit those who were not guilty. Sometimes these tests were fairly innocuous; for example, one test involved two parties being given candles of equal size that were lighted simultaneously. The individual whose candle lasted the longest was determined to have won their case. Other times, however, the tests were dangerous, and sometimes even deadly. One test required the accused to walk through large flames to see if their guilt would manifest as severe burns.

It was not until the twelfth century that juries re-emerged in the Western legal system. King Henry II created the earliest version of the English jury system by convening groups of regular citizens to decide disputes over land in secular courts (a notable change after centuries of the ecclesiastical system). However, unlike the modern jury, these jurors functioned more like investigators and were tasked with uncovering the facts of the case on their own, rather than listening to arguments presented in court. Although Henry II began the trend toward juries, it was his son, King John, who is generally credited with ushering in the modern jury system. Indeed, one of the most influential provisions of the Magna Carta, signed by King John, states: "No free man shall be captured or imprisoned or disseised of his freehold or of his liberties, or of his free customs, or be outlawed or exiled or in any way destroyed, nor will we proceed against him by force or proceed against him by arms, but by the lawful judgment of his peers . . ."With the Magna Carta established as foundational law, the jury system became more and more commonplace in England.

The expansion of the British Empire spread the jury system throughout Europe and also brought it to Asia, Africa, and eventually the American continent. Interestingly, while the jury system infiltrated nearly all corners of the world, many nations later took it upon themselves to abolish it. The jury system was abolished in Germany in 1924, Singapore and South Africa in 1969, and India in 1973. Today, even in those countries where the jury system still exists, it is used only sparingly. For example, in France, jury trials are only held for very serious crimes (specifically those that carry a minimum of ten years' imprisonment) and only in one specific court system, *the cour d'assises.* Overall, more than 90 percent of all jury trials in the world currently occur within the United States. Perhaps Americans tend to place the jury system in such vaunted esteem precisely because it is so uniquely American.

The right to a jury in a criminal trial is enshrined in the Sixth Amendment, which states: "In all criminal prosecutions, the accused shall enjoy the right to a speedy and public trial, by an impartial jury of the State and district wherein the crime shall have been committed." Likewise, Article III, Section 2 of the Constitution minces no words by providing: "The trial of all crimes, except in cases of impeachment, shall be by jury."

While the text securing the right to a jury is quite broad, important limitations do exist. The Supreme Court in <u>Baldwin v. New York</u> suggested that the right to a jury applies only when a defendant is charged with a "serious" offense, which it defined as a crime carrying a prison sentence of more than six months. Numerous criminal convictions mandate sentences of less than six months, including many types of drug offenses. In these cases, a defendant has no federally guaranteed right to a jury, meaning that their entire case can be heard and decided exclusively by a judge.

However, it's important to note that some states have protections for criminal defendants that are broader than federal law, meaning that juries in these states are still guaranteed even for "lesser" crimes. For example, California guarantees a right to a jury trial for all criminal cases carrying any possibility of imprisonment; no six-month threshold is required. This reflects an important concept of federalism that is worth mentioning—namely that federal law always sets the "floor" for civil liberties and protections, but states are always free to increase (not decrease) these protections if they so choose.

While most think of juries as being part of criminal cases, they are also used frequently in civil cases. Under the Seventh Amendment, jury trials are guaranteed for certain civil lawsuits: "In suits at common law, where the value in controversy shall exceed twenty dollars, the right of trial by jury shall be preserved . . ." Interestingly, very little is known about the curious twenty-dollar threshold. (For reference, twenty dollars in the year 1800 would be worth about four hundred in today's dollars.) The twenty-dollar requirement is so utterly inconsequential that it is often simply ignored by judges and legal scholars when discussing the Seventh Amendment.

Deciphering which civil cases warrant a jury trial and which do not is an extremely complicated exercise that regularly puzzles (and frustrates) even the most industrious law students. It suffices for our discussion to know that juries in civil trials are common, and that the use of juries in this context stands as a stark outlier among legal systems throughout the globe. In fact, the Unites States is the only country in the world to widely use juries in civil cases.

Most everyone already knows that a jury's ultimate responsibility is to listen to the evidence presented at trial and decide whether a defendant is "guilty" or "not guilty" in criminal cases, and "liable" or "not liable" in civil cases. Yet, the true role of the jury is actually a bit more specific. Juries are commonly referred to in law school classrooms as "fact-finders." In other words, jurors have the duty of sifting through all the evidence presented by both sides of the case to establish the truth. However, the jury has no role in analyzing the actual law. Rather, the judge instructs the jury on what the law says and explains how it must be interpreted. The jury then applies the facts of the case to the applicable law and determines guilt or liability.

Juries cannot hear all of the evidence, however. The jury may only listen to evidence that is legally admissible. Here, the judge once again has the important role of deciding what evidence a jury is allowed to hear and what evidence must not be disclosed. Many forms of evidence, such as hearsay testimony or a report from an unqualified person alleging to be an expert, will be excluded from trial. Other times, however, the question of admissibility is not so clear. Lawyers will often have vigorous "mini trials" on matters simply relating to what evidence is allowed to be presented to the jury. Overall, while juries serve a hugely pivotal role, trial dynamics involve a constant interplay between the powers of the judge and jury.

Finally, it's important to note that, in criminal cases, juries generally do not have any role in determining the punishment imposed on a defendant once they have been convicted. It is the role of the judge to determine prison sentences and other forms of punishment. By contrast, in civil cases, juries are usually responsible for deciding the amount of damages (i.e., financial compensation) to award the prevailing party.

Voir Dire

Okay, with our brief history and background information now established, let's get into the actual jury selection process.

"Voir dire" is the term used to describe the process of selecting a jury, and its rules and procedures can often be as strange as the term itself (it's French, pronounced "vwar deer"). During voir dire, lawyers from both sides will question prospective jurors to determine if they are biased or otherwise cannot be relied on to view the issues fairly. For example, if a prospective juror has previous knowledge of the facts of the case, a relationship to one of the parties to the case, an occupation which might lead to bias, or a previous personal experience similar to the case, that individual will likely be excused from jury service. This should make intuitive sense—after all, the jury for a murder trial should not include the defendant's grandmother, nor should a trial for arson include a jury member whose whole family was recently killed in a tragic house fire. Such individuals cannot be trusted to be impartial.

Unique problems arise when jurors are selected for high-profile cases that have garnered significant public attention, such as terrorist attacks or notable murders. In these cases, large segments of the society have already formed opinions of the case based on what they have seen on television or the internet. The psychological theory of confirmation bias suggests that humans tend to interpret new evidence in ways that confirm or support one's prior beliefs. When presented with evidence that challenges our preconceptions, we tend to fight it, or even ignore it outright. To help find jurors with a more neutral perspective, judges in high-profile cases will sometimes move the whole trial to an entirely different location where the case might not be as newsworthy. For example, in the Oklahoma City bombing cases, the trials were moved all the way to Denver, in part because the courthouse that would have normally housed the trials was seriously damaged in the blast. There is no doubt that selecting an impartial jury inside a courthouse that was still being repaired due to the defendants' alleged bomb would have been essentially impossible.

But what about cases that are popular throughout the nation, not just locally? Due to the rise of the internet and social media, the details of many high-profile cases now spread far and wide across the country, and the jury section process has struggled to adapt. Consider the relatively recent trial of Martin Shkreli, the founder of several pharmaceutical companies and known widely online as the "Pharma Bro." In 2015, Shkreli was heavily criticized when one of his companies obtained the manufacturing license for the drug Daraprim (used commonly by AIDS patients) and raised its price by 5,000 percent. After news broke of the gigantic price increase, Shkreli seemed to relish the criticism he faced, and even started flaunting his money on his popular Twitter feed and YouTube channel. At one point, Shkreli won an online auction for a special Wu-Tang Clan album, reportedly bidding over two million dollars. After securing the album, Shkreli commented during an interview that he would let Taylor Swift listen to it in exchange for sexual favors. Suffice it to say, Shkreli became widely despised, with countless news sources cataloging his misbehaviors and labeling him the most hated man in America. Several popular memes of Shkreli also began circulating throughout the internet on prominent websites and forums such as Reddit.

In 2017, Shkreli was charged with several counts of securities fraud (i.e., investment fraud). Before trial, more than two hundred prospective jurors were excused during voir dire, primarily because so many people were already familiar with Shkreli's antics and poor reputation. For example, let's look at the real-world questioning of the very first prospective juror in the case:

THE COURT: The purpose of jury selection is to ensure fairness and impartiality in this case. If you think that you could not be fair and impartial, it is your duty to tell me. All right. Juror Number 1.

JUROR NO. 1: I'm aware of the defendant and I hate him. I think he's a greedy little man.

THE COURT: Jurors are obligated to decide the case based only on the evidence. Do you agree?

JUROR NO. 1: I don't know if I could. I wouldn't want me on this jury.

THE COURT: Juror Number 1 is excused.

To really illustrate the point, let's look at a few more responses from the more than two hundred prospective jurors that were excused:

JUROR NO. 10: The only thing I'd be impartial about is what prison this guy goes to.

JUROR NO. 47: He's the most hated man in America. In my opinion, he equates with Bernie Madoff.

JUROR NO. 67: The fact that he raised the price of that AIDS medication, like, such an amount of money disgusts me. I don't think I'll ever be able to forget that. Who does that, puts profit and self-interest ahead of anything else? So it's not a far stretch that he could do what he's accused of.

JUROR NO. 77: From everything I've seen on the news, everything I've read, I believe the defendant is the face of corporate greed in America. You'd have to convince me he was innocent rather than guilty.

JUROR NO. 144: He kind of looks like a dick.

Needless to say, none of these jurors were selected in the Shkreli trial. After several weeks of voir dire, twelve purportedly unbiased jurors were eventually identified. Shkreli was found guilty of several counts of securities fraud and sentenced to seven years in prison.

Removals "For Cause"

If an attorney's questioning reveals that a prospective juror is biased in some way, that juror can be removed from the jury "for cause." Whether or not a prospective juror is sufficiently biased is typically decided by the judge. In addition to having preexisting opinions about the case or defendant (like the potential jurors in the Shkreli case quoted above), there are a few other common forms of bias that will quickly lead to a prospective juror being excused for cause. For example, being a police officer or having a close family relative who works in law enforcement will often result in a prospective juror being removed in criminal trials. The assumption is that these prospective jurors will be biased in favor of police testimony and reports. Additionally, blatant racism is usually an automatic disqualifier.

Here, we find a popular area of misinformation. Perhaps you've previously been summoned to jury duty and, knowing you want to get out of the tedious process, a friend offers up some super savvy advice: "Just lie and say you're a racist, or that you're an anarchist, or that you think all criminals should be put to death! They'll definitely let you off the hook!" Maybe that will happen. Or maybe they'll put you in jail. Courts make it abundantly clear to all potential jurors during voir dire that they are under oath. Lying while under oath is considered perjury, a criminal offense carrying potentially severe penalties. For example, in 2012, a man in Massachusetts received a two-year prison sentence after he was caught lying during voir dire. Regularly overseeing the voir dire process for thousands upon thousands of potential jurors over their careers, most judges are wise to every trick in the book to get out of jury duty. It's highly unlikely that any plan you hatch hasn't already been tried before. In short, you might get away with pretending to be biased during voir dire to escape jury duty, but you might also end up behind bars.

Other forms of juror bias are much less obvious than overt attestations of racism. Often, attorneys must ask tactful questions in order to elicit sufficient evidence to convince the judge that a prospective juror should be removed for cause. In questioning prospective jurors, attorneys are actually afforded surprising latitude; questions often probe deeply into private life, asking about religious beliefs, drinking habits, hobbies, jobs, romantic relationships, prior experience with the court system, experiences as crime victims, and even arrest records. Only minimal restrictions exist limiting the scope of questioning, which are typically enforced by the judge. One court decision from 1988, Connecticut v. Barnes, illustrates the extreme breadth of questioning allowed during voir dire. Here, the defendant had been charged with theft for stealing a family's Christmas gifts, and the court ruled that his attorney was entitled to ask prospective jurors about their "attitudes toward Christmas" during voir dire.

Before moving on, it's important to note that "bias" in a prospective juror is not necessarily a pejorative term. Sure, some prospective jurors might be outright racist, sexist, or xenophobic, but oftentimes bias simply means that someone is predisposed to view certain facts in a certain light. All of us are biased in some way or another; such is the result of a life lived amongst unique circumstances and situations. You don't necessarily have to be a "bad" person to be removed from a jury. Quite the contrary. For example, you may have once been a victim of sexual violence and now harbor extremely negative views of anyone even accused of a similar crime. That is a normal aspect of human psychology. Yet, even these forms of "innocent" bias can skew the outcome of a trial if the jurors are not properly removed.

Peremptory Challenges

In addition to removals for cause, there is another way to exclude a prospective juror, known as a "peremptory challenge." It's here that we encounter perhaps the most controversial aspect of the entire trial system. A peremptory challenge allows a party to exclude any prospective juror without the need for any reason or explanation—just *poof*, that juror is excluded. In contrast to removals for cause, which are unlimited, each party is only allowed a certain number of peremptory challenges, typically between three and ten, depending on the jurisdiction and the type of case. Given their limited supply, peremptory challenges are highly coveted, and significant strategy is involved in deciding when to use them.

The peremptory challenge has been critiqued for a wide variety of reasons, most prevalent among those being its potential to discriminate based on race. For much of American history, Black individuals were forbidden from serving on juries. Indeed, it was not until

1935 that the Supreme Court in <u>Norris v. Alabama</u> explicitly ruled that Black citizens must have an opportunity to serve. By the 1940s, the Supreme Court put forth the idea that the jury should represent a cross-section of the community from which it was selected. For many cities in the southern states with large Black populations (some even with majority Black populations), this meant that juries in these areas should start to see large proportions of Black jurors. Yet, such increased representation never manifested. For decades, juries remained mostly white, largely due to peremptory challenges striking Black jurors.

In the criminal system, particularly when a Black defendant is on trial, prosecutors have historically fought to keep Black individuals off of the jury. For example, in the 1965 case of <u>Swain v. Alabama</u>, an all-white jury in Talladega County, Alabama, convicted a nineteen-year-old Black man of raping a seventeen-year-old white girl. The man was subsequently sentenced to death. During voir dire, the prosecutor had used six peremptory challenges to remove from the jury all of the Black individuals eligible to serve. A review of records later revealed that not a single Black person had served on a criminal or civil jury in Talladega County for more than a decade.

The motivation for prosecutors to use peremptory challenges to strike Black jurors is fueled by the stereotype that Black individuals are frequently biased against the criminal justice system. While legal scholarship has worked to rebuff these claims, the O.J. Simpson acquittal in 1995 provided fodder for these arguments to grow. Although it was widely believed by the public that Simpson had murdered Nicole Brown Simpson and Ron Goldman, the majority-Black jury acquitted Simpson of the murder charges. Following the highly publicized acquittal, polls showed that views of the case were firmly split among racial lines: nearly 90 percent of white individuals believed Simpson was guilty, whereas only around 20 percent of Black individuals felt the same.

While Black jurors have been disproportionately the subject of peremptory challenges, white individuals have certainly been accused of their own biases, whether in favor of police and white defendants, or against Black defendants. In fact, jurors across all races and ethnicities have generally been thought to possess a favorable bias toward defendants who look like themselves. Race continues to play a salient role in jury selection, arguably above any other personal attribute. In fact, the abolishment of South Africa's jury system was due largely to the fact that the country's serious racial division meant fair jury trials would be very difficult.

Importantly, in the 1986 case of <u>Batson v. Kentucky</u>, the Supreme Court ruled that peremptory challenges cannot be used to exclude prospective jurors based solely on race. Thus, on paper, it is now illegal to exclude Black jurors via peremptory challenges specifically because of their race. In real-world practice, however, <u>Batson</u> did little to actually change the status quo. Under the so-called Batson Test, a party may object to an attorney's peremptory challenge if they believe it was used to exclude a prospective juror based solely on race. However, to rebut the objection, the other party's attorney need only offer a race-neutral reason for the dismissal of the prospective juror. Most lawyers are clever people who can easily craft an argument to explain that their peremptory challenge had nothing to do with race but was actually based on any number of other factors. Strategies for excluding Black jurors while still succeeding on the Batson Test are so common that some attorney training videos on YouTube actually offer advice on how to do it. Numerous studies conducted throughout the country have shown that Black individuals are still excluded from juries at disproportional levels.

The Great Façade in Jury Selection

For decades, the legal system has championed the voir dire process as a means to achieve an impartial jury. But is that really how attorneys are using the process? Short answer: *no way*.

It's important to understand that the abundance of effort devoted to jury selection is not necessarily in search of true impartiality. While the justice system might like to extol this concept, the whole idea is kind of a façade that masks the true intentions of attorneys. Attorneys are not expending significant resources in search of impartial truth seekers. Few lawyers are so virtuous—they just want to win. What lawyers are actually doing is striking jurors who they think will not be favorable to their side of the case, and arguing to keep those who will.

Overall, the voir dire process is typically used to secure a trial advantage more so than impartiality. The "winner" of voir dire will end up with a jury that is more favorable to their side of the case. The ability of attorneys to more or less handpick their jury has caused the voir dire process to turn into an incredibly important part of the trial process. Given its potential to offer a winning advantage, voir dire can sometimes consume as much time as the actual trial itself. In one notorious case involving an alleged murder by a prominent Black Panther member, lawyers examined more than one thousand prospective jurors over a four-month period before finalizing the jury.

CRASH COURSE

Jury Nullification

Perhaps more so than any other legal topic, learning about jury nullification makes law students think they are so much smarter than everyone else. Once they've heard about jury nullification, they think they've uncovered some kind of secret power to circumvent the entire legal system. Although a law school student body is never short on pretention and overinflated egos, they're kind of right on this one— jury nullification actually is a genuine, legal loophole.

As we have discussed, juries are traditionally instructed to act only as "finders of fact." Their role is to determine the truth of the evidence presented, and apply that evidence to the law as it has been explained by the judge in order to reach a verdict. The jury is never supposed to question the actual law itself. However, jury nullification is an exception to this principle. Under the theory of jury nullification, juries are actually permitted to return a verdict of "not guilty" or "not liable" even when they believe the defendant has violated the law. In other words, the jury nullifies the law that it believes is either immoral, or for whatever reason has been wrongly applied to the defendant.

Jury nullification has appeared consistently throughout our nation's history whenever the government has tried to enforce morally offensive or otherwise unpopular laws. For example, in the 1800s, northern juries practiced nullification in prosecutions brought against individuals who were accused of harboring slaves. During the Prohibition Era of the early 1900s, juries likewise used their nullification powers to acquit defendants who had violated alcohol control laws. Perhaps the most recent and notable example of jury nullification occurred in the case of Dr. Jack Kevorkian, who had assisted terminally ill patients with suicide. Known as the "mercy doctor," Kevorkian willfully admitted to euthanizing dozens of his patients who sought to end their lives, but he was nevertheless acquitted of murder charges by the jury under the doctrine of jury nullification.

The jury's power to nullify is truly awesome in that it is enforceable and cannot be questioned. As we have discussed, after a jury has returned a "not guilty" verdict, double jeopardy protections generally prohibit any retrial on the same charge. Thus, jury nullification can—both figuratively and literally—allow a defendant to get away with murder. Interestingly, however, a jury's guilty verdict or finding of liability can be scrutinized by the judge. If a jury finds that a defendant is guilty despite overwhelming evidence of innocence, the judge has the authority to step in and reverse the verdict. Allowing judges to reverse guilty verdicts and findings of liability protects defendants from malicious juries. This is an important distinction: juries can nullify the law to a defendant's benefit without scrutiny, but they cannot condemn a defendant absent good reason.

Over the last few decades, courts have become extremely opposed to jury nullification, discouraging it whenever possible. Some judges will actually take it upon themselves to exclude a juror during voir dire if they make mention of their intent to nullify. Many judges will also forbid attorneys from directly appealing to jurors to nullify the law. This aversion stems from the idea that informing jurors of their power to nullify could lead to anarchy, with laws being enforced idiosyncratically, all depending on the sympathies of a particular jury. At the same time, many also support nullification, arguing that it serves as an important mechanism for feedback. Nullification can signal to the government when laws have become out of step with society.

A Grand Jury Would Indict a Ham Sandwich
The Grand Jury System

There are actually two distinct jury systems in the United States: the trial jury, which is the "conventional" jury we just discussed, and also the grand jury. The grand jury does not determine guilt or innocence. Rather, its role is to examine the preliminary evidence against a potential defendant and decide whether criminal charges should be filed against them (i.e., whether or not they should be "indicted"). As such, the grand jury can be thought of as the "gatekeeper" of the criminal justice system. We'll take a more in depth look at the form and function of the grand jury in just a moment.

But first, a bold claim: Over the last few years, the grand jury has played a direct role in eliciting more public outrage and widespread civil unrest than any other aspect of our legal system.

In 2014, nationwide protests erupted after grand juries declined to indict the police officers responsible for the deaths of Michael Brown in Ferguson, Missouri and Eric Garner in New York City. Just a year later, a grand jury in Cleveland, Ohio again spurred outrage after declining to indict the officer that killed twelve-year-old Tamir Rice. Most recently, a grand jury in Louisville, Kentucky chose to indict only one of the several officers involved in the death of Breonna Taylor, and only for the crime of wanton endangerment, not murder.

With all this in mind, let's go ahead and take a look at what grand juries actually are, how they function compared to conventional trial juries, and what they have to do with ham sandwiches.

The Purpose of the Grand Jury

The purpose of the grand jury is a mightily venerable one. As articulated by the Supreme Court, the grand jury stands as the "referee between the Government and the people." The ultimate role of the grand jury is to decide whether or not enough evidence exists to initiate criminal charges against a potential defendant. If, upon review of the evidence, the grand jury finds probable cause that a crime has been committed, the accused will be indicted and the case will commence. By contrast, if the grand jury deems that the evidence is insufficient to indict a suspect, the investigation typically ends, and no actual prosecution takes place. It's important to stress that an indictment only means that the criminal trial process can begin; it is not the same as a conviction, which means a defendant has actually been found guilty. Convictions are generally the responsibility of the trial jury, whereas indictments are within the purview of the grand jury.

The grand jury is often the community's first contact with the government's criminal investigation. As the gatekeeper between criminal investigation and criminal charges, the grand jury serves the twin aims of bringing the rightfully accused to trial and shielding the innocent from unfounded prosecution. Thus, the grand jury has been referred to as both a "sword" and a "shield." The importance of the grand jury is so paramount that a citizen's right to one is enshrined in the first words of the Fifth Amendment: "No person shall be held to answer for ... [an] infamous crime, unless on a presentment or indictment of a Grand Jury ..." An "infamous" crime has been interpreted to mean a felony crime, which is where grand juries are most often utilized.

As you can see, the role of the grand jury is much different than that of the trial jury. Indeed, many important differences exist. Compared to trial juries, grand juries are usually bigger, more secretive, and much more one-sided.

Size

While grand juries are no doubt "grand" in their importance, they have historically also been larger than trial juries. The name "grand" is derived from the French word "big." Although you don't hear it too often, trial juries are sometimes referred to as "petit" juries—the French word for "small." Grand juries can have as many as twenty-three jurors, as opposed to the conventional six to twelve trial jurors. Also in contrast to trial juries, grand juries never need to be unanimous in order to indict a defendant. Depending on the jurisdiction, only between two-thirds and three-fourths of grand jurors must vote to indict.

Secrecy

Secrecy is a core characteristic of grand juries. This is where things begin to get a bit controversial. Grand jurors meet in a completely sealed-off environment, behind closed doors, with no judge, no press, no defendant (in many cases), and no lawyer other than the prosecutor. All documents and transcripts are restricted from public disclosure, and all jurors are sworn to secrecy, meaning that they cannot discuss any aspect of the process with the public, even after the grand jury finishes its service.

As a quick personal note, I can attest to the near-mystical level of secrecy afforded to the grand jury process. Back in 2015, I interned at the U.S. Attorney's Office for the District of Massachusetts, which serves as the prosecuting arm of the federal government for the entire state of Massachusetts. Throughout my time there, I picked up on the distinct taboo of merely speaking about grand juries among office personnel. With the office located in the federal courthouse, where grand juries were convened, I heard plentiful stories about secret passageways throughout the building used to shield grand jurors as they came and went. On one occasion, I made the poor miscalculation of going up the wrong flight of stairs and found myself standing in a waiting area reserved for grand jury proceedings. Aesthetically speaking, the whole room was cold, sparsely decorated, and painted in a bland off-white—a stark contrast from the otherwise opulent and marble-laden federal courthouse. Two armed agents of the U.S. Marshal Service stood guard in front of a door, behind which a grand jury was apparently convening. "What are you doing here?" one of the agents barked at me. Before I had a chance to answer, a prosecutor I recognized emerged from the hallway, papers strewn about in his hands. We locked eyes and he shot me an angry glare before entering the guarded door. "Uh, wrong stairs," I mumbled, quickly scampering back down from whence I came.

The grand jury that was convened for Michael Jackson's alleged acts of child molestation had particular trouble staying secret. Once the news leaked and the media caught wind that the proceedings were taking place, prosecutors became concerned about public interference (even acts of spying) in the courthouse. As a result, the grand jurors were secretly moved from the courthouse to an unknown location, causing the press to scramble across Santa Barbara County in search of them.

Grand juries have been kept in high secrecy ever since their inception, and many would argue for good reason. In <u>Douglas Oil Co. v. Petrol Stops Nw.</u>, the Supreme Court affirmed the need for secrecy in the grand jury and offered several justifications for it. First, without the assurance of secrecy, helpful witnesses might either hesitate to come forward or be less likely to testify "fully and frankly," knowing that the people against whom they testify could find out. Such witnesses would be vulnerable to threats or bribery. Second, individuals about to be indicted might flee upon hearing that a grand jury has been convened. Third, individuals who are merely accused, but not ultimately indicted, benefit from a lack of public scorn.

Occasionally, however, the veil of secrecy can be lifted, but it typically requires a court's specific approval. For example, a court in Louisville made the unprecedented move to not only allow grand jurors in the Breonna Taylor case to speak about their experience, but also ordered the release of some fifteen hours of recordings from the proceedings. The Attorney General of Kentucky attempted to fight the court's order, stating that such public disclosure would "destroy the principle of secrecy that serves as the foundation of the grand jury system." Nevertheless, the court disagreed and found that the case's unique public importance warranted the disclosure.

Although secrecy in the grand jury is well-established, problems can arise when it is combined with the inherent one-sided nature of the system.

One-Sidedness

We've already discussed how the prosecutor utterly dominates the criminal system. Perhaps nowhere else is this more apparent than in the grand jury system. In fact, the grand jury has been referred to as the prosecutor's alter ego.

It's important to emphasize that, unlike a trial, the grand jury system is not adversarial. The prosecutor and the jurors are the only entities involved—the defense side simply isn't present. A potential defendant has no right to be informed that grand jury proceedings have commenced, and they cannot appear before the grand jury unless explicitly subpoenaed. If a potential defendant does happen to be subpoenaed to testify, his or her lawyer cannot be present. The prosecutor will question the accused exclusively. (As a note, because the process is not adversarial, there is typically no voir dire process involved in selecting grand jurors.)

Above all, the most important factor in the grand jury's decision to indict is the evidence presented to them. But here's the catch: the prosecutor provides all of the evidence that the grand jurors will ever review. Shocking to most, in many jurisdictions, the prosecutor is not required to present evidence that is favorable to the accused, even if such evidence is within their possession. Additionally, many traditional evidentiary protections do not apply during grand jury proceedings. For example, hearsay evidence, which is prohibited at trial, can be presented to grand juries.

Returning to the sword and shield metaphor, there is a growing perception that grand juries have become the prosecutor's own sword and shield: a sword to be used in furtherance of the prosecutor's goals, and a shield to hide the prosecutor's activities from the prying eyes of the public.

Considering the immense prosecutorial control over grand jury proceedings, it should come as no surprise that jurors overwhelmingly choose to indict. Out of 162,351 cases presented to federal grand juries in 2010 (the most recent year for which statistics have been released), jurors declined to indict in only eleven cases. In other words, grand juries indict potential defendants over 99.99 percent of the time. It is this overwhelming trend toward indictments, coupled with the complete control of the prosecutor during grand jury proceedings, that led one unnamed New York attorney to opine in a 1979 newspaper that a prosecutor could persuade a grand jury to "indict a ham sandwich." The phrase was then repeated by the Chief Judge of New York State's highest court, Sol Wachtler, where it gained notoriety in the legal community.

Grand Juries in Cases of Alleged Police Misconduct

Historically, the grand jury process has been critiqued for allowing prosecutors too easy an avenue to indict defendants. Recently, however, the opposite criticisms have surfaced regarding grand juries convened to examine controversial police shootings. Many have accused prosecutors of using the grand jury system to purposefully exonerate officers by convincing the jury not to indict. For example, in Houston, Texas, local grand juries have cleared police of shooting civilians 288 times in a row.

In response to the grand juries failing to indict the officers involved in the high-profile cases of Michael Brown, Eric Garner, and Tamir Rice, and failing to indict on murder charges for Breonna Taylor, nationwide protests erupted as many accused the prosecution of deliberately sabotaging the process. For example, the Rice family released a statement accusing the county prosecutor of purposely manipulating the jury to orchestrate a vote against indictment. Opponents of current grand jury dynamics believe that prosecutors can use the system to trick the public into believing that it was the community who declined to indict the officers, when, in reality, the prosecutor controlled the proceedings to virtually ensure the outcome. Many also perceive a fundamental conflict of interest in allowing prosecutors to control grand jury proceedings against police officers. Prosecutors work closely with police officers on a daily basis; they are typically all on the same "team," with prosecutors relying on the police to feed them new cases. This potential for bias has actually caused a handful jurisdictions to remove local prosecutors from cases involving police misconduct, instead handing them over to state authorities.

Before wrapping up this topic, it's important to acknowledge, as always, that there are two sides to this story. To be sure, some do support the grand jury process as it exists today. For several decades, the Supreme Court has continuously supported the secrecy and prosecutorial control found in the system. As the threshold marker in deciding whether an actual criminal trial is warranted, some believe that it is appropriate for the prosecution to have the control needed to make the best possible case against the defendant; this ensures that all wrongdoers face justice. Additionally, many claim that the overwhelming number of grand jury indictments compared to non-indictments is simply a reflection of prosecutors electing to only take up cases for which they possess robust evidence. With regard to grand juries in police shootings, an argument also exists that non-indictments are a result of the unique aspects of the law more so than prosecutorial bias. Compared to average citizens facing murder charges, police officers are afforded broad legal protections when using deadly force, making it much more difficult for a grand jury to find probable cause that they have committed a murder under the applicable law. As one particularly extreme example, Missouri law allows police officers to use deadly force if they reasonably believe (1) it is necessary in order to make an arrest and (2) the suspect has committed a serious felony crime and has caused, threatened, or may cause serious physical injury. Operating under the parameters of such an expansive law, it would be more difficult for any grand jury, regardless of prosecutorial intent, to indict a police officer for murder compared to an average citizen.

Real Courtroom Drama Can Be Better Than TV
Wacky Courtroom Exchanges

There is a common perception that the law is bland and boring. To be sure, the dull and dense stereotype can often be true (have you ever tried to actually read the terms and conditions you sign every time you update your smartphone?). However, this book has (hopefully!) shown you many instances where the law can actually be quite interesting and weird. Sometimes, the law is even downright hilarious.

In the courtroom, where the law lives through human action, things can get the absolute wackiest. For many, the idea that the courtroom is occasionally disrupted with childish antics might come as a surprise. After all, television dramas like *Law & Order* portray the courtroom as a kingdom of seriousness, and the high-profile trials we watch on the news are rife with formalism and intensity. Most of the time, this is all true—the courtroom is typically a very carefully controlled environment. Court rules and regulations forbid food and drink, mandate that certain attire be worn, and often prohibit cell phones and other electronics. To enforce these rules, judges have the power to place individuals in criminal contempt (i.e., immediately put them in jail) for violating court procedures or otherwise offending the court with poor behavior. And yet, despite the plentiful rules in place to curb misconduct, and despite the sanctity and solemnness we have afforded to the courtroom, there are countless instances of shocking and outlandish behavior caught on record in the form of word-for-word courtroom transcripts. Nearly all courtroom interactions are transcribed by speedy stenographers and become part of the public record for that case.

The sheer volume of courtroom interactions will inevitably allow some shenanigans to slip through the cracks. More than fifty million court cases are filed throughout the country each year. The number of individual jurors, plaintiffs, defendants, attorneys, and judges who must continually interact with one another is enormous. As a simple matter of probability and human nature, bad behavior is bound to surface. As this book comes to a close, it is perhaps best to end with some levity. Let's now jump in and review a few particularly wacky courtroom transcripts.

Judge Bernie Bouchard and Defendant Darius Dabney, Hamilton County, Ohio

Darius Dabney, standing in a crowded courtroom with his attorney, was awaiting his turn to be heard for a probation violation. But there was a problem: the stench of marijuana pummeled the entire courtroom, described by witnesses as "smack-you-in-the-face overwhelming." Judge Bouchard, noticing the smell, asked where it was coming from. At first, no one admitted to possessing the marijuana. Judge Bouchard then asked the courtroom again, this time threatening to bring in drug-sniffing police dogs. Finally, Dabney admitted that it was him, prompting this ridiculous exchange:

MR. DABNEY: I smoked marijuana before I got here.
THE COURT: Okay. Well, do you have it on you?
MR. DABNEY: No, sir.
THE COURT: Well, it doesn't smell to me like burnt.
MR. DABNEY: I'm cool then.
THE COURT: You're safe, you think?
MR. DABNEY: I know I am.
THE COURT: What time did you smoke it?
MR. DABNEY: Shit, like since 9:00, 9:15. I'll be honest about that. I ain't going to hold you up. I just got out on a probation violation for a dirty piss, so I smoked this morning. I ain't going to hold you up. I ain't going to hold you up. It's me. I got—
THE COURT: What's your name? Do you remember that?
MR. DABNEY: I don't know that right now.
THE COURT: Okay. Why don't you come up here and have a seat so we can maybe—maybe we can—I don't care what your name is. Come on up. Maybe you can remember your name by the time you sit up here. Have a seat right over here.
COURT CLERK: Well, we have his attorney here.
THE COURT: You have Mr. Moore? [The Attorney]
MR. DABNEY: Yes, sir.
THE COURT: Okay. No, no, no. Right here. What's his name, Mr. Moore?
MR. MOORE: Dabney, Darius Dabney, Your Honor. He did answer to his name earlier, though. Judge, what happened with Mr. Dabney, he's here for a probation violation. He just recently got out for another

felony probation violation.

THE COURT: And celebrated.

MR. MOORE: Evidently so.

THE COURT: Yeah. Well, I don't think I can take a plea from him today because he's not of sound mind.

MR. DABNEY: Can I come back?

THE COURT: Yeah, you're going to come back, but here's the problem, you're going to stay with us for a couple days.

MR. DABNEY: What?

THE COURT: Yeah.

MR. DABNEY: Sir, I have my son outside. Like I really have my son. Like I got to pick up my son at 10:00, 11:00.

MR. MOORE: Your Honor, I did speak to him earlier and he knew his name and he knew essentially why he was here and that sort of thing. He didn't strike me as someone who was intoxicated. Judge, I know that he was kind of carrying on a little bit in the back there, but I think he was just having fun, essentially, is what it comes down to, Judge. I'm satisfied that he's ready to proceed.

THE COURT: Well, thank you for that, but I mean, he just admitted that he smoked marijuana right before he came to court.

MR. DABNEY: Oh my gosh. Like, Mr. Bernie-

THE COURT: It's Judge Bouchard, but that's okay, Mr. Dabney. You want to step on up here, Mr. Dabney. I'm finding you in contempt, sir, for coming to court high, wasting the Court's time, public defender's time, everybody's time that's getting paid here. You can't enter a plea because you're not of sound mind, so you're going to do a day in jail for that on contempt. Now, listen to me, Mr. Dabney. If you got it on you, it's going to be a felony when they strip you over there so I'll give you one last time to tell me if you have any unburnt marijuana on you. I'm giving you—oh, ah-ha!

[Defendant pulls a large bag of marijuana out of his pants.]

THE COURT: Okay. So, finally you came clean. If there's anything else, this is your opportunity. We're going to destroy it. Are you sure?

[Defendant pulls another large bag of marijuana out of his pants.]

THE COURT: Oh my lord. Anything else, I mean, because—

MR. DABNEY: No.

THE COURT: Mr. Dabney, I'm telling you—Now why would you do that? Why would you bring that much pot to court?

MR. DABNEY: I forgot it in my car, sir.

THE COURT: You forgot it in your underwear.

MR. DABNEY: I don't know, sir.

THE COURT: You don't know. Well, I don't know why you would do that either.

MR. MOORE: Well, Judge, I mean, it's—if he's impaired to the point that he can't take a plea, he's probably not thinking clearly.

THE COURT: Good point. Mr. Dabney, well, you know—

MR. DABNEY: Yes, sir.

THE COURT: You know what, I just want to tell you one thing. You know, at some point in your life all you have left is your word, okay, you know, and to be honest. You hear what I'm saying? You know, it's just so disappointing that, you know, you try to lie. I've been in court every day for twenty years as an assistant prosecutor, a magistrate, and a judge. And for you to think that I'm stupid and you're going to pull one over on me, I mean, that's just illogical. But you know what I appreciate in this courtroom is honesty, you know. If you can say 'I did something, I'm sorry, I learned from it,' that goes a longer way than 'no I didn't' and lying, you know. So, I mean, you did come clean, but it took a little coaxing, but that's better than you getting charged with a felony for bringing drugs into the jail. You know what I'm saying? So I hope that you at least learned from this and can be honest in the future.

MR. MOORE: Judge, he might not realize it, but he appreciates you giving him the opportunity to get rid of it.

THE COURT: Okay. We'll see you tomorrow morning. You're in contempt and doing a day in jail.

The exchange between Dabney and Judge Bouchard is emblematic of the discretion in the legal system that we have discussed throughout this book. Although Judge Bouchard, himself, did not have the authority to charge Dabney with felony marijuana possession (marijuana is still illegal in Ohio for recreational purposes), he could have easily sent the matter to one of the county prosecutors, who would have happily obliged the request of a judge. Instead, Judge Bouchard sentenced Dabney to a single day in jail for what was arguably just a boneheaded mistake.

Statistics do not paint a very rosy picture of incarceration rates in the United States. By far, the United States leads the world when it comes to putting people in jail, outranking even places like El Salvador, Rwanda, and Russia. Currently, there are more than two million people in our nation's jails—a 500 percent increase over the last forty years. These are serious statistics, and they should be treated as such. That said, such extraordinary numbers might belie the reality that many legal authorities are rational, good people simply trying to make their communities a better place.

Judge Bouchard appears to be one of those people. He gave every opportunity to Dabney to come clean about the marijuana he was possessing. And then, realizing that there was little benefit in undertaking a felony prosecution against Dabney, he decided to show some leniency. As explained by his very tactful attorney, Dabney was likely too inebriated to fully realize what he was even doing. Using his discretion, Judge Bouchard figured the best course of action was to dole out a minor form of punishment, but not enough to upend Dabney's whole life.

Judge Wanda Drusch and Defendant Ernie Wayne Terteltge, Gallatin County, Montana

Ernie Wayne Terteltge was in court for an omnibus hearing (a type of pretrial hearing where various evidentiary and scheduling matters are taken care of) in connection with charges for resisting arrest and fishing without a license. From the very onset of the hearing, Terteltge instantly became combative and launched into bizarre and bombastic rhetoric that hardly made any sense at all. Judge Wanda Drusch became so flustered with Terteltge that she had to walk out of the courtroom for a few minutes to collect herself.

THE COURT: Mr. Terteltge, you're here in court today because you were charged with—
MR. TERTELTGE: I am here in court today because I am making a special visitation. This is not an appearance, only spirits appear. Living men, living persons make special visitations. That's why I'm here; to make sure that you guys don't danger my truthful proper name.
THE COURT: Do you still live at 28 Flying Eagle in Manhattan?
MR. TERTELTGE: That is a storage unit that I sleep in from time to time.
THE COURT: All right.

MR. TERTELTGE: I live in myself in this body. I am the living man.

THE COURT: Mr. Terteltge, you were here—you were seen by Mr. Klutz—did you apply for the public defender?

MR. TERTELTGE: They can only speak fictitious legalese to you. I speak natural living man's English to you, it's called common English. That is the only thing that I will do.

THE COURT: That's fine.

MR. TERTELTGE: There will be no legalese used here.

THE COURT: You were charged on the 31st of August of 2013 with obstructing a police officer in violation of 457302. You were also charged on the same day with resisting arrest in violation of 457301 of the Montana Code.

MR. TERTELTGE: Those men were charged by me right back by staging an overthrow of the Constitution of 1789, an overthrow of the Bill of Rights, an overthrow of my rights to forage for food as a natural living person who was in hunger. I was searching for something to put in my stomach as I am recognized to be allowed to do by universal law. That has nothing to do with your corporate fiction. They violated everything. And furthermore, for your knowledge, they violated Judge Holly Brown's Title 26 United States Code ruling which I went before her and prevailed on 21st March 2011, EPO 9-58AS, the case number wherein she evidenced that I am not a taxpayer because I am not a federal citizen, federal law trumps state law at every turn. I have nine judge rulings to that end and that trumps state law. I am the living man and I have the right to forage for food when I'm hungry.

THE COURT: All right. But you're here on different charges.

MR. TERTELTGE: That is what stands.

THE COURT: This is not Holly Brown's courtroom.

MR. TERTELTGE: Ma'am, you can argue this all day long, you're operating on a corporate fiction.

THE COURT: I'm telling you, you're here on some charges, which were filed. Number one—

MR. TERTELTGE: I do not understand those charges.

THE COURT: Number one—you keep interrupting me and I am going to charge you with contempt and you'll go to jail.

MR. TERTELTGE: What contempt. If the court has spelled C-O-N-N, I know that conning-

THE COURT: Sir, I said be quiet until I get—

[Bailiff approaches Mr. Terteltge]

MR. TERTELTGE: Don't touch me, you ain't a god. Don't you judge me, I am the living man protected by universal law.

THE COURT: You keep shouting and you are going to be charged with contempt and you're going to go to jail.

MR. TERTELTGE: You have already contempted this court by what you are trying to get done here.

THE COURT: I told you I would if you didn't quit talking—

MR. TERTELTGE: These are the living witnesses to what you're trying to do. You are trying to create a fictitious fraudulent action. You are trying to build the Federal Reserve by securitizing an all caps commercialized name and notifying them that they—

THE COURT: Sir! Sir! Would you remove him from the courtroom, officer?

[Bailiff approaches Mr. Terteltge again]

MR. TERTELTGE: If you touch me, you will violate natural law. Do not come near me. I am protected by the law.

THE COURT: Then shush, shush—

MR. TERTELTGE: Do not tell me to shut up! I am the living natural man and my voice will be heard! That is the Jolly Roger. That thing you call the American flag with the gold fringe around it is the Jolly Roger and you are acting as one of its privateers.

THE COURT: Okay. You're here on the charge of resisting arrest, Mr. Terteltge.

MR. TERTELTGE: I'm here by special visitation.

THE COURT: Right.

MR. TERTELTGE: I do not understand any charges. I only understand universal law and the right to live—to live in peace and to live as I need to.

THE COURT: You pled not guilty in this—

MR. TERTELTGE: I never plead, animals plead, sounds like bah, oink oink.

[Mr. Terteltge makes animal sounds]

THE COURT: I have a paper with your signature on it, sir.

MR. TERTELTGE: It says prime evidence standing right through it. You bring forward all natural forms of evidence that I'm not prime evidence. I am the living soil, the dirt, the water and the air has its own voice does it not? It also supports all forms of life does it not? I am a part of that life. I am not your corporate fiction.

THE COURT: Sir?

MR. TERTELTGE: Do not danger me.

THE COURT: You're here today on an omnibus hearing. You've already pled not guilty—

MR. TERTELTGE: I am here by special visitation to see through that you do not danger my natural living man's name.

THE COURT: Are you prepared to tell the court, if you wish to go to trial on this matter?

MR. TERTELTGE: This is a trial. Tell this is not—

THE COURT: No, this isn't a trial.

MR. TERTELTGE: Here is my jury—

THE COURT: This is an omnibus hearing, sir.

MR. TERTELTGE: You cannot produce a jury of my peers because all juries are selected from a pool of registered voters and the instant a person registers to vote their natural ability is averred to comprehend natural law has been dissolved and turned into fiction. There cannot be raised a jury of my peers. It cannot be done.

THE COURT: Excuse me for just a moment.

MR. TERTELTGE: No way. Get back here and finish this. Hey. Hey. Get back here and finish this. The Judge has left the courtroom, there you go.

[Judge Drusch leaves the room]

Each and every day, judges are faced with unruly defendants in court. Emotions will naturally run high in a courtroom, particularly in criminal court. Defendants are extraordinarily stressed, with their liberty and freedom at stake. Most defendants have spent days, weeks, or even months in the local jail awaiting their court date. Some may have been falsely accused, while others might be in the throes of a psychotic episode. As a steward of the justice system, it is incumbent on a judge to remain levelheaded and accept even the most vitriolic of defendants.

But judges are still human beings. When flustered, wise judges, like Judge Drusch, will leave the room and allow themselves a moment to regain composure before dealing with defendants like Mr. Terteltge. Other judges will simply have a bailiff remove the defendant from the courtroom if they begin to act out of turn, and allow them to return later. Other times, however, judges will let their guard down and allow a defendant's antics to get the best of them. No one knows this better than Judge Bryant Durham.

In a small county courthouse in rural Georgia, defendant Denver Fenton Allen was before Judge Bryant Durham for a pretrial hearing. Allen was in prison after being convicted of making terroristic threats. While serving his sentence, he allegedly beat a fellow inmate to death and was charged with murder. While defending against the murder charge, Allen had disagreements with his publicly appointed attorney. During a pretrial scheduling hearing, Allen expressed to Judge Durham that he wanted to change his attorney before his trial. Almost instantly, the exchange between Allen and Judge Durham devolved into complete and utter chaos. The transcript from this particular hearing is regarded as being the most vulgar courtroom exchange ever caught on record. It is so vulgar, in fact, that its full contents were deemed too inappropriate for this book.

Below is just a quick snippet of the transcript (it gets *so* much worse). If you should find yourself interested, the full transcript can be found at my website, www.maclenstanley.com, along with more details about what happened to Judge Durham.

THE COURT: Do you understand that?

MR. ALLEN: Getting mad, ain't you?

THE COURT: Stupid.

MR. ALLEN: Or red-faced?

THE COURT: Listen!

MR. ALLEN: Now, you're calling me stupid.

THE COURT: Listen! Yes, I am.

MR. ALLEN: This is kangaroo court.

THE COURT: You know what, you have a constitutional right to be a dumbass.

MR. ALLEN: Why don't you jump up on the stand and—

THE COURT: You have a constitutional right to be a dumbass!

MR. ALLEN: —and jump around like a fucking kangaroo, you dumb bastard?

THE COURT: A constitutional right to be a dumbass!

Attorneys Questioning Doctors at Trial

During the trial process, expert witnesses are often required. These witnesses are designated as experts in their particular field of work, and their testimony is used to help the jury understand certain complexities of a case. Many legal battles include certain aspects that are simply too complicated for the average jury to understand without assistance. Professionals of all kinds can be used as expert witnesses at trial. For example, structural engineers can be used to show how and why a building collapsed; computer scientists can explain how a bank left their software vulnerable to hacking attacks; and an accountant might offer their opinion that a hedge fund mismanaged investor funds.

Expert witnesses are unique in that they are allowed to review all of the available evidence in a case and offer their opinions, inferences, and even conclusion. By contrast, other witnesses (referred to as "lay witnesses") are typically only allowed to state factual accounts of things they actually experienced. As an example, imagine that a defendant is being sued for causing a car crash that left the plaintiff with serious neck injuries. The plaintiff alleges that the defendant was speeding and rear-ended his vehicle on the highway. A witness to the accident is called to testify and explains to the jury that she heard tires screeching loudly just before the impact. While this lay witness testimony is helpful for the plaintiff, an automotive engineer is also called to testify as an expert witness. The engineer reviews skid marks from the scene, as well as the amount of metal denting on the plaintiff's trunk caused by the impact, and concludes that the defendant was traveling at ninety miles per hour, well above the speed limit.

As you can see, the testimony from an expert witness can be an incredibly powerful tool. Each side of a dispute typically hires their own expert, with each expert (not surprisingly!) reaching a different conclusion. Both sides also have the opportunity to question each other's experts (during the "cross-examination") and make strategic efforts to diminish their credibility. Ultimately, the jury will be tasked with deciding which expert was more persuasive.

Among the many types of expert witnesses used at trial, doctors are the most common. Virtually every personal injury case will require a medical expert to offer their opinions regarding the severity of the plaintiff's injuries. Should the plaintiff prevail, the jury will then use this information to decide how much financial compensation should be awarded. Criminal cases also frequently involve expert medical testimony, most often during homicides. Here, medical experts will review autopsy reports and offer their conclusions about how exactly a victim died.

In reviewing transcripts of expert witnesses at trial, doctors tend to have the most ... attitude. Perhaps doctors don't like lawyers all that much, or perhaps there exists some latent competitiveness between these two "top" professions. Whatever the reason, doctors tend to respond to a lawyer's questioning with the most snark compared to the members of any other profession. This is particularly true when being questioned by the opposing party's attorney. Remember, the opposing party is typically trying to undermine the credibility of the doctor.

According to an old article published in the Massachusetts Bar Association Lawyers Journal, the following are real-world examples of doctors quipping at attorneys in court:

ATTORNEY: Do you recall the time that you examined the body?
DOCTOR: The autopsy started around 8:30 p.m.
ATTORNEY: And Mr. Denton was dead at the time?
DOCTOR: If not, he was by the time I finished.

ATTORNEY: Now Doctor, isn't it true that when a person dies in his sleep, he doesn't know about it until the next morning?
DOCTOR: Did you actually pass the bar exam?

ATTORNEY: Doctor, how many of your autopsies have you performed on dead people?
DOCTOR: All of them. The live ones put up too much of a fight.

ATTORNEY: Doctor, before you performed the autopsy, did you check for a pulse?
DOCTOR: No.
ATTORNEY: Did you check for blood pressure?
DOCTOR: No.
ATTORNEY: Did you check for breathing?
DOCTOR: No.
ATTORNEY: So, then it is possible that the patient was alive when you began the autopsy?
DOCTOR: No.
ATTORNEY: How can you be so sure, Doctor?
DOCTOR: Because his brain was sitting on my desk in a jar.
ATTORNEY: I see, but could the patient have still been alive, nevertheless?
DOCTOR: Yes, it is possible that he could have been alive and practicing law somewhere.

CONCLUSION

Please hold back your tears as we endeavor to wrap up this book. What a wild ride it has been!

Throughout our many discussions, we have learned some pretty startling truths about the law, from police using civil asset forfeitures to fund lavish parties, to women being forced to look at ultrasounds of their unborn fetuses before having an abortion. The laws we have discussed have also spanned numerous domains, including criminal law, civil law, tort law, employment law, constitutional law, contract law, property law, and courtroom procedure. As mentioned in the Introduction, it is my suspicion that you will begin to notice these legal topics throughout your everyday life. In fact, this may have already happened to you. Have you seen an op-ed about felony murder appear on your newsfeed? Has a friend posted about the Electoral College? Have you heard someone critique the merits of <u>Roe v. Wade</u>? From this book, you should find yourself better able to not only notice the legal discussions that surround you, but also engage with them, intelligently and with nuance.

While the topics covered have been varied, it is my hope that you were able to identify some common threads woven throughout the book. For example, we have frequently discussed the grey nature of the law and the surprising amount of subjectivity and discretion involved in legal analyses and interpretation; we often touched on the concept of federalism and the vast differences found between each state's laws and those of the federal government; and we focused on the differing mental components that form prerequisites to crimes and torts. But, perhaps most of all, I hope that you have recognized the undeniable human element of the law.

Judges, lawyers, and politicians often speak of the law like it's part of the natural order of things, as if the law regulates human action in the same way chemical bonds command atoms to attract or repel. Not so. The reality is that human beings have envisioned, authored, and upheld the law. If you have ever met a human being, you already know that we are highly prone to being emotional, irrational, hypocritical, biased, self-serving, and weird—just look at the courtroom transcripts in the last topic! As much as we might extol its sanctity, the law cannot help but be a reflection of us.

As it stands today, every aspect of the law necessitates human input and intervention—from the legislator who votes to enact a law, to the police officer on the street who effectuates an arrest, to the prosecutor who uses her discretion to bring charges, to the grand jury that chooses to indict, to the jurors selected by the attorneys during voir dire to deliberate and reach a verdict, and to the judge who ultimately imposes a prison sentence. By the same token, it is only through human action that unjust laws can be dismantled or amended. Each one of us has the power to influence the law, albeit indirectly. Because our government functions as a republic (and not a true democracy), our power ultimately lies in prompting our representatives to act, whether through votes or social pressures. Sometimes, however, citizens can take a more direct role in effecting change.

In 2017, Jenny Teeson, a woman from Minnesota, was in the middle of a divorce when she found a flash drive containing numerous videos taken by her husband. The videos depicted him having sex with her and penetrating her with objects as she lay nonresponsive on their bed. Unknown to her at the time, her husband had been drugging her and sexually assaulting her while she was incapacitated. Teeson handed the videos over to the police and her husband was charged with criminal sexual conduct in the third degree, which prohibits sexual acts with someone who is incapacitated. But, surprising even the judge and prosecutor, a legal loophole existed that shielded the husband from criminal liability for those exact actions. Specifically, the loophole exempted spouses from liability when performing sexual acts on their partners who are incapacitated. The charge was dropped within hours of being filed.

Bewildered and not wanting other victims to suffer a similar fate, Teeson endeavored to have the law changed and the loophole repealed. For nearly two years, she initiated multiple advertisement campaigns to bring attention to the loophole, petitioned members of the Minnesota legislature to repeal the law, and even shared her personal story on the floor of the state capitol. Teeson was in attendance at the capitol when it was announced in 2019 that the legislature had voted to repeal the loophole. Reportedly, as the announcement was made, all legislators present turned to applaud her.

Perhaps in a not-so-distant future, sophisticated computer algorithms will eliminate the need for human input in the justice system. Machine learning and artificial intelligence might be able to analyze numerous pieces of evidence and reach optimal and equitable conclusion. Simulation-based computer programs will calculate social variables to deduce the best laws to achieve a harmonious and productive society. Or, perhaps, the law will remain forever tethered to humans—something that cannot be replicated by a series of 0s and 1s. Can any computer program, no matter how advanced, ever truly compute the greyness that currently fills the law? Can a computer practice discretion in the way that a human can? And to that point, do greyness and discretion actually complement our notion of justice?

This is a question worth considering. Throughout this book, discretion has been framed largely as a positive aspect, but is that truly the case? Should Judge Bouchard have let Darius Dabney largely off the hook for the two large bags of marijuana he brought into the courtroom? Is that really fair for the countless individuals who are arrested and charged with felony drug possession each and every day?

One area where discretion has received particular scrutiny is during the sentencing phase, where judges typically have wide latitude to decide how long a defendant should be sentenced to prison. In the 1980s, disparities in prison sentencing became a national concern. Defendants charged with the very same crime were receiving wildly disparate sentences. Most often, those with more severe sentences were racial minorities. To combat this issue, Congress passed the Sentencing Reform Act of 1984, which created very specific sentencing guidelines for federal judges (with many states following suit with their own guidelines). Essentially, once a defendant was found guilty, judges were required to input different variables into a "sentencing calculator," including the specific crime that defendant committed and their criminal history. This calculation would then spit out the prison sentence. With the passage of the Sentencing Reform Act, all of the discretion in sentencing that judges once possessed suddenly vanished.

This seemed to work for a few years, but then a new set of problems started to surface.

With judges bound by the rigid guidelines, they were now unable to demonstrate leniency where it may have been warranted. Gradually, the guidelines became viewed as draconian and unfair, mandating sentences that were too severe for plaintiffs that may have simply made a boneheaded mistake or found themselves in questionable straits, but were trying desperately to turn their life around. This was particularly true for defendants convicted of drug crimes, with federal sentencing guidelines demanding especially severe sentences for drug offenses.

In 2005, the Supreme Court ruled in <u>United States v. Booker</u> that the sentencing guidelines were no longer mandatory, but merely "advisory." Federal judges were instructed to "consider" the calculated guideline sentence, but were not obligated to actually abide by them. In other words, federal judges were once again allowed discretion in their sentencing. This is how the law currently stands today. And once again, controversy has emerged.

In 2017, the United States Sentencing Commission released a report showing that Black men who commit the same crimes as white men receive federal prison sentences that are, on average, nearly 20 percent longer. Significant disparities still persisted even after controlling for a wide variety of typical sentencing factors, including age, education, citizenship, weapon possession, and prior criminal history. With <u>Booker</u> once again affording discretion to judges, disparate sentencing patterns have reverted back to the problematic state of the 1980s. Discretion is inherently a double-edged sword: it can impart leniency when needed, but at the cost of others suffering disproportionally. Given imperfect human nature, discretion will always allow bias to infiltrate the justice system. So, how do we combat the problems of discretion? The truth is, no one knows. Legal scholars are currently wrestling with these very questions.

Many attempts have been made to include bias training, particularly unconscious bias, into mandatory continuing education courses for attorneys across the country. Most prosecuting agencies have also implemented similar training seminars. Whether these tactics prove effective, the data has yet to manifest.

Above all, I hope this book has given you the tools to start *thinking* about the law. You have now read enough about the black letter law to achieve a basic understanding of many foundational tenets of our legal system. Even more importantly, you have been primed to think about our legal system, in all of its weird glory. We have seen how imperfect human reasoning has shaped our legal system, examined why the law has turned out this way, discussed how the law is actually applied, and questioned what form it might take in the future.

Our discussion on abortion provides a good example of how you might go on to think about the law. At the onset, we spent some time discussing the black letter law of Roe v. Wade. However, we dedicated the brunt of our effort towards analyzing the "right to privacy" standard that formed the backbone of the case, discussing where the standard came from and how it ended up being used to protect abortions. We then examined the inherent subjectivity involved in the "undue burden" and "viability" standards, and discussed how different states have capitalized on ambiguities to achieve their own versions of justice. Finally, we looked at what might happen if Roe were eventually overturned.

As you encounter legal discussions in the future, you should approach them in the same way. Ask yourself: Why might that law be the way that is it? How can subjectivity and discretion affect the real-world influence of the law? Is the law applied differently across different states? How might the law evolve in the future? These are important questions that everyone should be asking of the laws that control their daily lives, particularly those laws that are really *weird*.

Acknowledgments

Some people describe writing a book as a magnificent and soul-elevating process, like giving a flawless birth, hitting a grand slam, or watching a butterfly fart a rainbow—but that's not exactly how this book played out. The truth is that the law is difficult and complex, and articulating the law in a way that's both enlightening and enjoyable for you to read was not an easy endeavor. That said, and in my humblest of opinions, I think I have arrived at something very special here—but not without the help of a few outstanding people.

Many thanks to Anna Vande Velde, April Bosch, and Professor Scott Westfahl for their help in reviewing this book and allowing me to bounce ideas off of their gigantic brains.

Additionally, I extend my largest token of gratitude to my wife, who, for no less than two years, was forced to listen to countless iterations of this book and every (bad) idea under the sun. A true testament to her warrior spirit, she managed to feign interest throughout.

In fact, I dedicate this entire book to her—Ashleigh Stanley.

Bibliography

CASES

Almeida-Sanchez v. United States, 413 U.S. 266 (1973).

Baldwin v. New York, 399 U.S. 66 (1970).

Batson v. Kentucky, 476 U.S. 79 (1986).

Berman v. Parker, 348 U.S. 26 (1954).

Biscan v. Brown, 160 S.W.3d 462 (Tenn. 2005).

Brandenburg v. Ohio, 395 U.S. 44 (1969).

California v. Ciraolo, 476 U.S. 207 (1986).

Chaplinsky v. New Hampshire, 315 U.S. 568 (1942).

Chapman v. United States, 365 U.S. 610 (1961).

Connecticut v. Barnes, 547 A.2d 584 (Conn. App. Ct. 1988).

County of San Diego v. San Diego NORML, 165 Cal. App. 4th 798 (Cal. Ct. App. 2008).

Cruise-Gulyas v. Minard, 918 F.3d 494 (6th Cir. 2019).

Davidson v. City of Westminster, 649 P.2d 894 (Cal. 1982).

Donoghue v. Stevenson, UKHL 100 (1932).

Douglas Oil Co. v. Petrol Stops Nw, 441 U.S. 211 (1979).

Ekas v. Clackamas County Sheriff's Office, No. CV 09-831 AC (D. Or. July 20, 2009).

Gamble v. United States, 139 S. Ct. 1960 (2019).

Gardner v. Village of Chicago Ridge, Ill. 219 N.E.2d 147 (Ill. App. Ct. 1966).

Gonzales v. Raich, 545 U.S. 1 (2005).

Griswold v. Connecticut, 381 U.S. 479 (1965).

Gutierrez v. Cobos, 841 F.3d 895 (10th Cir. 2016).

Hartzler v. City of San Jose, 46 Cal. App. 3d 6 (1975).

Heath v. Alabama, 474 U.S. 82 (1985).

Hester v. United States, 265 U.S. 57 (1924).

Illinois v. Caballes, 543 U.S. 405 (2005).

Javins v. First National Realty Corp., 428 F.2d 1071 (D.C. Cir. 1970).

Katko v. Briney, 183 N.W.2d 657 (Iowa 1971).

Katz v. United States, 389 U.S. 347 (1967).

Kelo v. City of New London, 545 U.S. 469 (2005).

Kentucky v. King, 563 U.S. 452 (2011).

Kline v. 1500 Massachusetts Avenue Apartment Corp., 439 F.2d 477, (D.C. Cir. 1970)

Kyllo v. United States, 533 U.S. 27 (2001).

Lawrence v. Texas, 539 U.S. 558 (2003).

Liebeck v. McDonald's Restaurants, No. CV-93-02419, 1995 WL 360309 (D. N.M. Aug. 18, 1994).

Lozito v. City of New York, No. 101088/12 (N.Y. Sup. Ct. July 25, 2013).

L.S. v. Peterson, No. 18-cv-61577, 2018 U.S. Dist. LEXIS 210273 (S.D. Fla. Dec. 12, 2018).

Mary M. v. City of Los Angeles, 54 Cal.3d 202 (1991).

Miller v. California, 413 U.S. 15 (1973).

Morgan v. Virginia, 328 U.S. 373 (1946).

Nome 2000 v. Fagerstrom, 799 P.2d 304 (1990).

Norris v. Alabama, 294 U.S. 587 (1935).

Ohio v. Bryner, 9th Dist. No. 18CA011257 2018-Ohio-3215.

Oliver v. United States, 466 U.S. 170 (1984).

People v. Aiken, 828 N.E.2d 74 (N.Y. 2005).

People v. Beardsley, 113 N.W. 1128 (1907).

People v. Hernandez, 393 P.2d 673 (Cal. 1964).

People v. Hernandez, 624 N.E.2d 661 (N.Y. 1993).

People v. Ingram, 492 N.E.2d 1220 (N.Y. 1986).

PepsiCo, Inc. v. Leonard, 88 F.Supp. 2d 116 (S.D.N.Y. 1999).

Planned Parenthood v. Casey, 505 U.S. 833 (1992).

Ramos v. Louisiana, 140 S. Ct. 1390 (2020).

Rodgers v. Kemper Construction Co., 124 Cal. Rptr. 143 (1975).

Roe v. Wade, 410 U.S. 113 (1973).

Silverthorne Lumber Co. v. United States, 251 U.S. 385 (1920).

South Dakota v. Opperman, 428 U.S. 364 (1976).

Stanley v. Georgia, 394 U.S. 557 (1969).

State v. Ellis, 841 S.E.2d 247 (N.C. 2020).

State v. Rodriguez, No. CF-2017-00205 (D. Okla. 2017).

Stoner v. California, 376 U.S. 483 (1964).

Swain v. Alabama, 380 U.S. 202 (1965).

Terry v. Ohio, 392 U.S. 1 (1968).

Thiel v. S. Pac., Co., 328 U.S. 217 (1946).

Tison v. Arizona, 481 U.S. 137 (1987).

United States v. $63,530.00 in U.S. Currency, 781 F.3d 949 (8th Cir. 2015).

United States v. Approximately 64,695 Pounds of Shark Fins, 520 F.3d 976 (9th Cir. 2008).

United States v. Booker, 543 U.S. 20 (2005).

United States v. Cephas, 254 F.3d 488 (4th Cir. 2001).

United States v. Darby, 312 U.S. 100 (1941).

United States v. Flores-Montano, 541 U.S. 149 (2004).

United States v. Lee, 274 U.S. 559 (1927).

United States v. Lopez, 514 U.S. 549 (1995).

United States v. Miller, 425 U.S. 435 (1976).

United States v. Moalin, 973 F.3d 977 (9th Cir. 2020).

United States v. Roman, No. 14-4126 (D. Utah 10th Cir. June 23, 2015).

United States v. Williams, 504 U.S. 36, 47 (1992).

Vasquez v. Residential Investments, Inc., 118 Cal. App. 4th 269 (Cal. Ct. App. 2004).

Vaughan v. Menlove, (1837) 132 Eng. Rep. 490.

Warren v. District of Columbia, 444 A.2d. 1 (D.C. 1981).

Weeks v. United States, 232 U.S. 383 (1914).

Whole Woman's Health v. Hellerstedt, 136 S. Ct. 2292 (2016).

STATUTES

8 U.S.C. § 1357 (2020).

18 U.S.C. § 921 (1990).

21 U.S.C. § 841(b)(1)(A) (1970).

21 U.S.C. § 844 (a) (1970).

21 U.S.C. § 960(b)(1) (1970).

Cal. Health & Safety Code § 123464.

Colo. Rev. Stat. § 18-1-704.5 (2016).

Fla. Stat. Ann. § 776.012.

Fla. Stat. Ann. § 776.013.

Mass. Ann. Laws ch. 278, § 8A.

Magna Carta art. 39, June 15, 1215.

Md. Code Ann., Crim. Law § 2-305.

Me. Rev. Stat. Ann. tit. 17-A, §104 (2007).

Mich. Comp. Laws Ann. § 750.520d (2018).

Mo. Rev. Stat. § 563.046 (2017).

Tenn. Const. Art. IX, § 3.

Tex. Code Crim. Proc. Ann. art. 59.01–59.14.

Tex. Penal Code Ann. § 9.42 (West 2019).

Yamhill County, Or., Code § 5.08.110 (2019).

NEWS & ARTICLES

Bennice, Jennifer A., and Patricia A. Resick. "Marital Rape: History, Research, and Practice." Trauma, Violence, & Abuse 4, no. 3 (2003): 228–46.

Brenan, Megan. "61% Of Americans Support Abolishing Electoral College." Gallup News, September 24, 2020.

Eisenberg, Ann M. "Removal of Women and African-Americans in Jury Selection in South Carolina Capital Cases, 1997- 2012." Northeastern University Law Review 9, no. 299 (2017).

Freivogel, William H. "For Phelps County: Seizing Suspects' Assets Is Like 'Pennies From Heaven.'" Pulitzer Center, February 24, 2019.

https://pulitzercenter.org/reporting/phelps-county-seizing- suspects-assets-pennies-heaven.

"Grand Jurors Can Talk Publicly about Breonna Taylor Case, Judge Rules." WLKY, October 20, 2020. https://www.wlky.com/article/ grand-juror-can-talk-publicly-about-breonna-taylor-case-judge-rules/34427973.

"Jury Selection with Jack McMahon All 1 Hour and 1 Minute." YouTube. DATV Productions, 2015. https://www.youtube.com/ watch?v=Ag2I-L3mqsQ&feature=youtu.be&t=3420.

Krauss, Elissa, and Martha Schulman. "Myth of Black Juror Nullification: Racism Dressed Up in Jurisprudential Clothing." Cornell Journal of Law and Public Policy 7, no. 1 (1997).

McArdle, Megan. "Let Roe Go." Washington Post, July 3, 2018.

Motivans, Mark A. "Federal Justice Statistics, 2013 – Statistical Tables." Bureau of Justice Statistics (2013): 11–12.

Pinkerton, James. "Hard to Charge: Bulletproof Part 3." Houston Chronicle, n.d. http://www.houstonchronicle.com/local/item/ Bulletproof-Part- 3-Hard-to-charge-24421.php.

Ross, Janell. "Two Decades Later, Black and White Americans Finally Agree on O.J. Simpson's Guilt." Washington Post, March 4, 2016.

Schmitt, Christopher. "Plea Bargaining Favors Whites, as Blacks, Hispanics Pay Price." San Jose Mercury News, December 8, 1991.

"Seale Jury Seated After 4 Months of Questioning." New York Times, March 12, 1971.

About the Author

Maclen Stanley is a Harvard Law School graduate and holds an Ed.M. in Developmental Psychology from Harvard's Graduate School of Education. He is a practicing attorney and currently runs a law firm dedicated to pursuing claims of sexual assault, sexual harassment, and gender discrimination. He lives in Los Angeles with his wife, who is also a lawyer and just happened to be sitting next to him during his very first law school lecture. They argue less than you'd think.

CONNECT WITH MACLEN STANLEY

Sign up for Maclen's newsletter at
www.maclenstanley.com/newsletter

To find out more information visit his website:
www.maclenstanley.com

Twitter:
www.twitter.com/MaclenStanley

Instagram:
www.instagram.com/maclenstanley

Facebook:
www.facebook.com/groups/203082128080296

BOOK DISCOUNTS AND SPECIAL DEALS

Sign up for free to get discounts and special deals
on our bestselling books at
www.TCKpublishing.com/bookdeals

CPSIA information can be obtained
at www.ICGtesting.com
Printed in the USA
BVHW042240300522
638482BV00002BA/4